Crossing Fandoms

Paul Booth

Crossing Fandoms

SuperWhoLock and the Contemporary Fan Audience

palgrave
macmillan

Paul Booth
DePaul University
Chicago, Illinois, USA

ISBN 978-1-137-57454-1 ISBN 978-1-137-57455-8 (eBook)
DOI 10.1057/978-1-137-57455-8

Library of Congress Control Number: 2016947220

Printed on acid-free paper

This Palgrave Macmillan imprint is published by Springer Nature
The registered company is Macmillan Publishers Ltd. London

To Kate: the Dean to my Sam, the Sherlock to my Watson,
the Tennant to my Capaldi…

Acknowledgments

I am grateful to a great number of people who have been supportive during the writing of this book. First and foremost, my most sincere thanks to all the fans who spoke with me about *Supernatural*, *Doctor Who*, *Sherlock*, and *SuperWhoLock*. This book would not have been possible without their candor and enthusiasm. Thanks to all the artists who gave permission to use their *SuperWhoLock* work. Special thanks to Martina Dvorakova, who patiently answered many questions about the history of *SuperWhoLock*. I am also grateful for the conference organizers who took the time to chat with me—Robbie Bourget from Gallifrey One and Adam Malin from Creation Entertainment were extremely helpful, and I appreciate their time. Thanks also to Fatenah Issa and Lynn Zubernis, who introduced me to Robbie and Adam, respectively. Thanks also to Zach Walsh, Holly Walsh, and Jon Petrie for hosting me when I stayed in London.

I first learned about *SuperWhoLock* from my student Nistasha Perez, and I am incredibly grateful for her passion and interest in the subject. My other students—especially those in my Fandom courses—have been equally engaged, and I am thankful for their thoughtful discussions over the years. DePaul University Research Council provided funding and the IRB provided resources for the research on this book, and it would not have been possible to write it without their help. A portion of Chap. 3 was previously published as "The Cultural Lives of Doctor Who: Celebrations, Conferences, Conventions" for *Antenna,* found at http://blog.commarts.wisc.edu/2013/12/03/the-cultural-lives-of-doctor-who-celebrations-conferences-conventions/. I presented parts of this book at the 2015 Fan Studies Network Symposium, and I am grateful to the organizers—Lucy

Bennett, Bertha Chin, Bethan Jones, Richard McCulloch, Tom Phillips, and Rebecca Williams—as well as my fellow panelists and attendees for the feedback. In particular, Kristina Busse and Alena Karkanias offered invaluable advice as I worked through some of the issues of this book. I also presented parts of this work at the University of Georgia and I am grateful to Shira Chess for organizing and Alison Alexander, Alexandra Edwards, James F. Hamilton, Jessica Hennenfent, Elli Roushanzamir, Nandita Sridhar, and Wes Unruh for attending. I am particularly grateful for Alex Edwards and James Hamilton for their comments during the discussion. Alex also kindly put me in touch with Amanda Brennan at Tumblr, and I am grateful for her insights as well. Fan studies is a fruitful and energizing discipline, and I am proud to work with some incredible colleagues across the world. Extra thanks to Ashlyn Keefe, whose comments on the final draft were extremely helpful in editing, and without whose keen eye this manuscript would be much weaker.

Working on a book for a program like Palgrave Pivot has been a fantastic academic experience—it is thrilling (and a bit scary) to know that the words I am writing now have just a few months before publication. I finished the book on the 52nd anniversary of *Doctor Who* and turned the manuscript in when the 2016 *Sherlock* special aired. I suspect that the final publication will happen around the season finale of *Supernatural*'s 11th season. My gratitude to everyone at Palgrave, especially Felicity Plester, Sophie Auld, and Sneha Kamat Bhavnani.

Thank you to my family for the support as I worked on the book—especially my wife, Katie, who may have had her fill of fan conventions for awhile. My great appreciation to Slinky, Rosie, Gizmo, and Black Kitty, without whom I would have no bellies to rub nor ears to scratch.

Contents

List of Figures

CHAPTER 1

Introduction: *SuperWhoLock* Fandom: Fandoms Crossed

Abstract This introduction to Crossing Fandoms describes *SuperWhoLock*—a fan-created amalgam of the television series *Supernatural*, *Doctor Who*, and *Sherlock*—as a symbol of contemporary digital fandom. Fans have created SuperWhoLock from the characters and narratives of the three cult texts. The consequences of today's mainstreaming of fandom means that fan work is more popular than ever. Yet, even as these three shows' universes create unique canon ideas, they still must stay tethered to the original text(s) in specific and meaningful ways. Thus, *SuperWhoLock* is not just a fan text; it is also a particular practice from which we are able to discern fan work in the digital age.

Keywords *SuperWhoLock* • Fandom • Fan-brand • Transmedia • Fan work

In a 2014 article, Laura Byrne-Cristiano makes a startling pronouncement:

> Fans of *Supernatural*, *Doctor Who*, and *Sherlock* have been talking about *SuperWhoLock* for years. Now thanks to an unprecedented deal, the idea will become reality. According to a joint press release issued by the CW and the BBC, "Having heard for years from the fans of our respective shows that they see the possibility of the crossover of our universes, we have decided to make this a reality.["][1]

P. Booth, *Crossing Fandoms*, DOI 10.1057/978-1-137-57455-8_1

This announcement must have come as a shock to stalwart fans of the three shows Bryne-Cristiano mentioned, many of whom may never have heard of *SuperWhoLock* (Fig. 1.1). According to the article, the idea first formed in the mind of fan favorite actor Mark Sheppard, who appears in both *Doctor Who* and *Supernatural*. Fans waited with baited breath for news of the premiere until they looked at the article's date (01 April) and realized that they had been had. *SuperWhoLock* would continue to remain a dream.

Of the scores of comments on the article, many readers seem to have been taken in, and some were actually quite angry that the article was not true. Reviewing some of the comments critically reveals some of the passions of *SuperWhoLock* fandom. Commenter Bad Wolf writes, "so this JUST now popped up on my facebook news feed, and i actually sent it to a few fellow SuperWhoLockians, then i read the comments about it being a joke, and i had to re-message them all correcting my blunder. it was awful, we were all so excited.:/." Casey McKim notes, in all caps, that "YOU PEOPLE ARE THE WORST I WAS SO EXCITED ABOUT THIS I COULDN'T EVEN HANDLE IT AND THEN I REALIZED IT WAS A JOKE AND IT WAS THE MOST DISAPPOINTING MOMENT EVER WHY WOULD YOU DO THAT TO ME WHY." And while Griffin

Fig. 1.1 *SuperWhoLock*, by cakeartist77 (http://cakeartist7.deviantart.com/art/Superwholock-364094678)

thought that the whole article was a joke, writing that *SuperWhoLock* is "one of the stupidest ideas [she has] ever heard," Byrne-Cristiano comments back: "Believe it or not, it's a gigantic thing on Tumblr[;] that's where we got the idea from."

Indeed, *SuperWhoLock is* a thing, whether or not Griffin or others think it is ridiculous.[2] *SuperWhoLock* is a fan-created amalgam of the television series *Supernatural* (WB 2005–2006, CW 2006–present), *Doctor Who* (BBC 1963–1989, Fox/BBC 1996, BBC-Wales 2005–present), and *Sherlock* (BBC 2010–present), and, as I argue in this book, represents a symbolic coming together of fandom in the digital age. Each of these shows has characteristics that develop from its historical moment. Harvey notes of *Doctor Who* and *Sherlock* that "as well as existing in relationship to each other, both programs exist in relation to the wider mediascape, in which their histories are necessarily implicated."[3] *Doctor Who* has an over 50-year-old history in a UK context; *Supernatural* is an American television series with a passionate fandom; *Sherlock* is the most recent show but is based on a series of mystery stories written over a 100 years ago with a centuries-old fan base. Steward writes of *Sherlock* that it is an "invention and product of television and its history rather than simply contemporary media."[4] Stein and Busse's description of *Sherlock as* a "transmedia web of paratexts and intertexts that bring Sherlock and his world into continued being," seems a perfect phrase to describe *SuperWhoLock* as well.[5] I want to augment these points by showing how *SuperWhoLock* should be understood as an invention and product of digital media and fandom, rather than just a product of these three traditional television media texts.

This is a book, therefore, about this fan-created text; but it is also a book about the way different fan audiences come together—online and in person—in this era of mainstreamed fandom. In some ways, *SuperWhoLock* recalls Matt Hills's term "trans-fandom," wherein multiple fan audiences interact with today's cult media products (and with each other) in ways that span texts and boundaries, "moving across different fandoms... moving across these different forms of fan knowledge."[6] *SuperWhoLock* utilizes cult icons, symbols, themes, and meanings from *Supernatural*, *Doctor Who*, and *Sherlock* in various ways, within different fan cultures, and toward different effects (Fig. 1.2).

Canonical information from these different series constructs a completely new narrative. Usually (although given the fluidity of the content, "usually" is often anything but), the brothers Sam and Dean Winchester from *Supernatural* are on a hunt, and are put in contact with Sherlock

Fig. 1.2 The author's homemade Funko Pop *SuperWhoLock* collection (Photo by the author)

Holmes and John Watson from *Sherlock* to help as experts. If the enemy is too immense, the Doctor from *Doctor Who* might pop in to offer help (or silliness). Often love triangles (or quadrangles) form between the characters. Often hearts or arms are broken. Often stories end in humor, or pain, or triumph, or tragedy.

In this book, I analyze the phenomenon of *SuperWhoLock*, arguing its relevance to digital fandom as a metaphor for the fluid and multifaceted presentation of fandom in an era of fannish mainstreaming. Indeed, although traditional media forms are becoming digital in *content* and *form*, they continue to be dominated by voices of mainstream ideology—the "fanboy auteur" that Suzanne Scott describes as controlling much television and film content (e.g., Russell T Davies, J.J. Abrams, Ron Moore) is precisely that: male (and white and cis-gendered).[7] Contemporary online digital media, however—media like web series[8]—are increasingly becoming shaped by more feminine and diverse voices—voices that, as I describe, are instrumental in the construction of *SuperWhoLock*.

SuperWhoLock is a completely fabricated text; but for followers of this fictionalized but accepted crossover, it is a specific manifestation of the popularity and mainstreaming of fandom today.[9] Scholars have been discussing for over two decades how fandom has become a more visible and more popular identity, although there is often a pejorative or negative association with the term and concept from many circles.[10] Yet, even within fannish circles, fandom of different texts is hierarchized: as Hills notes of *Twilight*, many fans of other fan texts look down upon or stereotype fans of the vampire romances.[11] Elsewhere, I have argued that fans of created texts like *SuperWhoLock* or *Inspector Spacetime* (a TV-show-within-a-TV-show on *Community*) "create the text they are fans of" by "linking the texts ... with the practices learned from other fan communities."[12] For fans of "created texts" like these, fans become media creators in their own right through pastiche, recombination, and replication of content. It is not entirely re-reading cult texts, nor it is quite re-reading fandom itself.[13] Rather, the creation of *SuperWhoLock* becomes a type of transgenic text in which new fan practices subtly change readings of fannish texts.[14]

SuperWhoLock is a fluid nexus of multiple fandoms, texts, and meanings. Busse and Hellekson have referred to fan fiction as "works in progress" that foreground the constant process of revision and critical reading that exists in the context of writing and reading fan fiction.[15] In contrast, I believe *SuperWhoLock* demonstrates "progress in works": rather than seeing a "work" (or text) as a central organizing category, which presupposes that boundaries exist surrounding the work in the first place, I see *SuperWhoLock* as a continual process with no central work upon which fans expand. There is no "center" to *SuperWhoLock*, and the bounds of the text extend beyond the canon ideals of the original three texts. Through an analysis of *SuperWhoLock*, I will argue that fan identities in the digital age are similarly "in progress," and constantly shifting within and outside the (artificial) boundaries placed on fan context. At the same time, there is a tension between the actualization of *SuperWhoLock* and the desire to keep it a closed system—a self-contained text under the fans' control and away from the industry. If fans of *SuperWhoLock* want their text to exist, it is usually in their own "head-canon" and not onscreen. If fandom is always a "work in progress," then *SuperWhoLock* is forever a work on the verge.

The importance of this analysis lies in the way fans are discursively constructed by the spaces in which they reside. In the digital world, these spaces may seem to be increasingly moving online (to sites like Tumblr, Twitter, Facebook, and WattPad).[16] Yet, sites of offline fandom are growing, as the popularity and mainstreaming of fan activities become both more acceptable and more marketable. Mainstreaming fandom runs the risk of hiding the less acceptable types of fan engagement, as Francesca Coppa notes:

> So now, more than ever, it is important to remember that fandom is made of people, and that fandom is beautiful, because fandom's in danger of being owned: our work, our communications, our relationships to and with each other. Fandom is more than its economic/revenue potential. If fannish participation is reduced to "likes" and "reblogs," if technology keeps drawing our attention to official Tumblrs and Twitters and YouTube channels (who will get paid for all the eyeballs they bring, and if even fan-made content becomes a source of industry revenues), if all of fandom starts to look like Comic-Con, i.e. an industry convention disguised as a fan convention, we run the risk of reducing all fans to followers.[17]

It is important to view all sides of the fan experience, from the most regulated to the most free, from the most commercialized to the most independent. Indeed, while focusing on the identity issues of fandom has been explored in previous fan studies literature, my aim in this book is to expand and develop this exploration of fan identity construction, positioning fan identity through its own textual appropriation.[18] *SuperWhoLock* becomes a comment on fans' own identities. That is, *SuperWhoLock* is a fan-created text that relies on a meta-knowledge of fandom.

This is not the first exploration of a fan-created text. Both Matt Hills and Lincoln Geraghty have discussed "Questarian" fandom, or fans of the television series within the film *Galaxy Quest*.[19] As mentioned above, I have also analyzed fandom of the show-within-a-show *Inspector Spacetime*.[20] However, *SuperWhoLock* is different than the others, in that *SuperWhoLock* fans have had to poach the canon of their texts from other shows; both *Inspector Spacetime* and *Galaxy Quest* are fictional but exist in the diegetic universes of the shows from which they emerged (the television series *Community* and the film *Galaxy Quest*, respectively). But there is *no* explicit *SuperWhoLock* canon; no crossover has intertextual, other than some moments in each of the shows where inter-textual references crop up (a character in *Supernatural* is named Amy Pond, also the name of a companion of the Eleventh Doctor, the Doctor has dressed up as Sherlock Holmes at times). The fact that fans of *SuperWhoLock* have explicated the connections between the three cult shows *without there being that text* becomes a mechanism for the way that fans build connections between fan cultures, a fandom to itself.[21]

Ultimately, then, this book—like *SuperWhoLock* itself—is making a number of interrelated, intertextual arguments. At a textual level, I want to examine *SuperWhoLock* as a truly *digital* text. In the rest of this introduction, I will discuss the history of *SuperWhoLock*, uncover some of the ways it rests on an inherent understanding of the digital media environment, and focus on what I am terming the "intra-transmedia" characteristics that undergird its construction. Intra-transmediation is the sense that transmedia characteristics exist inside a single text; that transmediation is a function not of the externality of texts to one another, but to the methods and means that fans use to cohere them together.[22] The concept builds on previous concepts of transmediation and my own concept of "intra-textuality" wherein the cohesion of a transmediated text emerges via close connections within multiple media spaces.[23] In this sense, I am building on work that I have previously done in *Playing Fans* to analyze *SuperWhoLock* as an exemplar of a new type of fan fiction, the GIF (graphics interchange format) Fics .[24] I extend this argument in this book to look not just at Gif Fics, but also at how Gif Fics, Gif sets, Gifs, fan fiction, artwork, and videos work together to create a sense of wholeness within a diverse canon.

At a slightly larger level, then, I move this discussion of *SuperWhoLock* onto notions of fandom itself. If the digital environment is facilitating a greater variety of fan activities, and fostering a fannish space for crossover texts to actualize, then fandom itself becomes a site of intra-transmediation. But because *SuperWhoLock* is an amalgamated text, it is an exemplar of the fact that fandom itself is a diverse, heterogeneous group. In order to examine how sites of fan activity help determine fan identity, I move from the digital landscape to the physical, from Tumblr to convention. In Chap. 2, I focus on the "Super" of *SuperWhoLock*, examining the way fans of *Supernatural* engage commercial enterprises for their fandom. In Chap. 3, the *Who* is revealed, as I describe the interaction of *Doctor Who* fans within *SuperWhoLock* fan circles. In Chap. 4, the *Lock* is opened up through an analysis of *Sherlock* fandom and its response to *SuperWhoLock*.

Given this organization, it may appear that I am actually contradicting my earlier point about trans-fannish activities; that is, because each chapter of the book ostensibly focuses on a *single* fan audience, I appear to be artificially separating the "Super" from the "Who" from the "Lock." In response, I would argue this "separation" is anything but, as *SuperWhoLock* itself is *artificially disparate*. The intra-transmedia characteristics of *SuperWhoLock*—the way that a single text can appear transmediated via the combinatory power of the crossover texts within it—paradoxically erase and create boundaries around the original three texts. Although *SuperWhoLock* is its own entity, it also requires disparate understandings of *Supernatural*, *Doctor Who*, and *Sherlock* for full effect. Thus, although one might argue the cohesion of *SuperWhoLock as a text*, it is in the points of rupture *between* the three requisite texts where the different fan audiences make meaning.

Fandom is discursively funneled into particular channels, and this book attempts to uncover the different meanings that *SuperWhoLock* can generate—and thus to understand the way different fan audiences both come together and divide themselves. To do this, I analyzed fan reactions to, and interest in, *SuperWhoLock* and other fan audiences at the *Doctor Who* convention *Gallifrey One* held in February 2015, the *Sherlocked* convention held in London in April 2015, and the Chicago *Supernatural* convention held in October 2015. In order to make sure the interviewees' voices were accurate, I emailed (whenever possible) transcripts of the interviews to the speakers in order to establish clarity and transparency with them. The fans I interviewed were often hyper-aware of their own experiences, and many were critical not just of the convention spaces they were at, but also of the types of fans they saw there. Most often, though, the fans I spoke with were highly engaged with my work and self-effacing: when told I was writing a book about *SuperWhoLock*, fans, and fan conventions, Mary (a longtime fan and convention-goer) responded, "Well, we *are* crazy," both echoing but also mocking contemporary discourses.

By using a cross-analysis of different fan conventions, I investigate commonalities and differences across different styles of fan convention and fan identities, in order to analyze the mainstream discursive construction of fandom. To put it simply, I am curious to explore the different "vibes" of unique fan audiences, and how those vibes "came together" or interact within interpretations of *SuperWhoLock*. Just as Lincoln Geraghty looks at the massive, multi-fandom Comic-Con as a site of fan identity construction, and Lynn Zubernis and Katherine Larsen examine the Creation *Supernatural* convention as way of showcasing a particular fan audience, so too do I focus on the role of the convention in determining fandom.[25] For instance, the *Doctor Who* convention *Gallifrey One* is entirely fan-run while the *Supernatural* convention is organized by Creation Entertainment, a for-profit company that also manages *Star Trek*, *Teen*

Wolf, *Vampire Diaries*, and *Stargate* conventions,[26] and the *Sherlocked* convention is a co-production of a television studio and a corporate body. This book will focus on the different expectations and cultures revealed within each of these spaces.[27] Fan conventions reveal both fans' playfulness with their fandom, as well as fan controversy and conflict. Each chapter explores the tensions within and outside the *Super*, the *Who*, and the *Lock* fan cultures.

History of *SuperWhoLock*

According to Nistasha Perez, a researcher working on Tumblr fandom, *SuperWhoLock* lacks a definitive start date, but "once the idea of combining the fandoms was formed, Tumblr's focus on sharing allowed people to reblog the resulting creations with a push of a button."[28] *SuperWhoLock* is a mainly Tumblr-based fandom (although there are *SuperWhoLock* works across the web in various guises: fan fiction on fanfiction.net and ArchiveOfOurOwn.org, videos on YouTube, art on DeviantArt, etc.). Although, Perez is right that there is no "start" to *SuperWhoLock*, it does have a date which can be marked as a "beginning." According to Google Trends, Google's search for mentions online, the first inklings of *SuperWhoLock* appeared in January 2012 (Fig. 1.3). The graph does not represent absolute numbers on searches, but reflects how many searches relative to total Google searches for the term over time.

In fact, the site shows that in December 2011, there was zero search interest, compared to July 2014, which is the highest point (100) of search

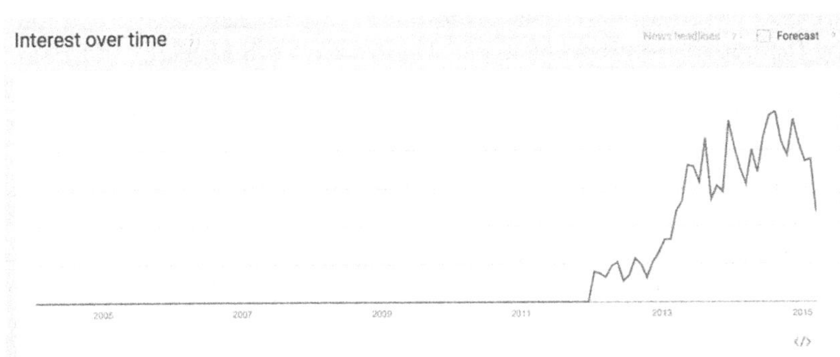

Fig. 1.3 *SuperWhoLock*, Google Trends, screenshot

interest. In January 2012, there was an 18% search interest in the term relative to July 2014. In 2015, there are multiple *SuperWhoLock* fan groups online—one ("Superwholockians: Ganking Demons and Solving Crimes in the Tardis") on Facebook mentioned by a student I interviewed, Amy,[29] has almost 13,000 members.[30] Google Trends only measures searches, however, and people rarely search for things without an impetus. The earliest *SuperWhoLock* work I could find on Tumblr was from 30 December 2011 (Fig. 1.4). Note that *SuperWhoLock* is already in the tags for the post, indicating that the title has either been created or is in the process of being concretized.

This particular Tumblr post, created by prettiestcaptain, has been reblogged over 6500 times. I got in touch with the author of this Tumblr post, Martina Dvorakova, who directed me to an even earlier post that was later taken down (Fig. 1.5).

In an email conversation, Amanda Brennan, a Content and Community Associate at Tumblr (and *SuperWhoLock* enthusiast) and I discussed tagging and fan classification on the site. Tags are an important element of Tumblr posts, and tagging various forms of #SuperWhoLock or #SWL are crucial ways of tying together a disparate community of fans. She notes that people tag for a variety of reasons—personal organization on their own blog, to make their content visible to others, to participate in fandoms or communities, or to add additional context to the post at hand. While Tumblr executives are reticent to release numbers (my questions about how many people tag or how much reblogging there is were ignored), the most shared posts tend to be the ones with multiple, and various, tags.

The centrality of this Gif set for *SuperWhoLock* has been confirmed by Brennan. I should note that, given the format of these texts, reproducing them in a book is problematic. These are what both Perez and I have called "Gif Fics," or moving Gifs.[31] A Gif is a small image file that rapidly layers images on top of one another, emulating a cinematic style of image juxtaposition.[32] A Gif Fic juxtaposes multiple moving images in a particular order like a comic strip, creating a narrative flow and animated style. However, "in print the images are still, but online all four of these images animate the characters mouthing versions of the lines written below. Each of these four images encapsulates that particular moment in the original text."[33] Thus, in print here, one will not be able to see the complete "story" each of these Gif Fics tells.

Fig. 1.4 *SuperWhoLock* 30 December 2011, by prettiestcaptain (http://prettiestcaptain.tumblr.com/post/15029266128)

I emailed with Dvorakova to ask more about her experiences making some of the earliest *SuperWhoLock* texts, and her response indicated how fluid its creation was:

> The crossover was something I noticed people talk about back then. Some people I followed mentioned putting these three shows together and I think there were already a few graphics floating around the site. I definitely

Fig. 1.5 *SuperWhoLock*, by Dvorakova (Reblogged at http://supernaturalapocalypse.tumblr.com/post/47164080621/ceiphiedknight-shadows-and-starlight)

> wouldn't say it just occurred to me, because there were a few people talking about it before and who gave me the idea to mix the show in a Gif set. It sparked my interest, I decided to give it a try myself and I discovered that the shows indeed fit together well.[34]

Dvorakova also noted some of the reasons why the shows seemed to fit so well together.

> I think it's because of the similar dynamics of the shows. ... In all three shows the characters solve problems and crimes, be [they] supernatural or

> not, so it's easy for the fans to think of a plot that could include characters from all these shows....[For] example, both *Supernatural* and *Doctor Who* introduced werewolves, which means in both universes werewolves are real and therefore they can easily be put together. One episode of *Sherlock* is devoted to the infamous hound, and with some imagination and alternations, you can easily turn the hound into a werewolf and voilà, you have a case they can all work on.[35]

There are a number of salient points made here. First, *SuperWhoLock* seems to have emerged through *fannish dialogue*, not top-down textual construction. That is, unlike other fandoms, including fandoms of the three requisite texts, which emerges for a *text* as it is *created*, *SuperWhoLock* appears to have been a fannish *discussion* which then manifest in fannish *practice*.

Second, there are multiple rationales for why *SuperWhoLock* "works," despite the disparate nature of the texts. In point of fact, each of the three texts that make up *SuperWhoLock* does not quite fit with the others in significant ways. In a Todorovian sense, *Sherlock* does not quite fit into the "marvelous" genre that *Supernatural* and *Doctor Who* exist in, where supernatural events become a reality (*Sherlock* seems to be the opposite; in which reality imposes rationality on the supernatural). From a production standpoint, where *Doctor Who* and *Sherlock* are both made by the BBC, *Supernatural* (made by the CW) does not quite fit; similarly, the "Britishness" of the two BBC shows is countered by the overt Americana of *Supernatural*.[36] And in many ways, *Doctor Who*'s long-standing, transmediated, and ongoing narrative arcs are different from the 3 seasons of *Sherlock* and the 11 seasons of *Supernatural*.[37] Each text is unique in some way, and yet somehow, they all seem to fit together somewhat naturally, as Dvorakova describes. The unique elements of each are the things that bind them—each features a white male protagonist (or two) who is troubled and emotional; each features story arcs as well as monster of the week episodes; each has a strong fan audience. *SuperWhoLock*—despite being composed of disparate texts—coheres as a whole, the sum of which is more than the parts.

Finally, there are semantic elements of the text that replicate across *SuperWhoLock*. Each of the shows does have its own unique iconography, but the icons are different *enough* that they fit together in the same *SuperWhoLock* universe. For instance, in Fig. 1.6, outside Holmes and Watson's residence at 221B Baker street sit both the TARDIS (the Doctor's

Fig. 1.6 *SuperWhoLock*, by Pop-Roxx (http://pop-roxx.tumblr.com/post/15794122295/because-there-arent-nearly-enough-superwholock)

time and space machine, in which he lives) and the Winchester brother's Impala, in which they spend most of their time crisscrossing America. This early example of *SuperWhoLock* depicts the actual or symbolic homes of the protagonists of the three shows neatly synched together in a tableau that illustrates both the naturalness of the scene (this could literally be a photograph of a street) and the diegetic implausibility (the uncanny nature of seeing a TARDIS outside Baker Street echoes similar semantic cross-overs in *Doctor Who*, for instance, where the Doctor dresses as Holmes).

SuperWhoLock encapsulates the particular "cult" properties of all three shows as they relate to one another. The similar ideologies of all three texts meet through these common characteristics: characters that can travel great distances, "alien" or strange protagonists, and the discovery of fantastic worlds that are made normal. Fans can get involved in *SuperWhoLock* by watching any of these shows and then imaginatively entering this shared universe. The reverse is also true: a *SuperWhoLock* fan I spoke with, Amy, "started watching *Sherlock* because of *SuperWhoLock*." This type of "fandom osmosis" occurs when someone watches *SuperWhoLock* and learns about a show they may not have seen previously.[38]

These texts function as a corollary for understanding the liminal relationship between fans and the media industries. The connections between the series occur not just because of the three show's common elements, but also because of the open-ended nature of each show's narratives. As Perez describes:

> Since the crossover is a fan creation, there is no single writer, director, or powers-that-be to say what happened and what didn't happen. Such freedom creates an open universe for fans to work in, ones where Dean can be a sniper or characters are forced to go undercover. Open universes act as loose frameworks for fan creators who are then free to create their own unique canon: from a plethora of ideas comes unlimited universes.[39]

Yet, even as these textual "open universes" create "unique canon" ideas, they still must stay tethered to the original text(s) in specific and meaningful ways. *SuperWhoLock* is not just a fan text; it is also a particular fan practice. According to Pat, a fan I interviewed at the Sherlocked convention in London, *SuperWhoLock* fans are "very much like the hero that they follow. You're attracted to the people who are most like you. So depending on whom the Doctor is, you'll see a change over in fans. With Matt Smith there was a lot of—well, how he is, exuberant. But I think now with Peter Capaldi, the fandom is calming down, a slight maturing." Another fan with whom I spoke at Sherlocked, Ben, augments Pat's analysis: "the Doctor and Sherlock aren't too different in character—there's a lot of similarities that appeal to both audiences." But of course, as the Doctor changes, so too does the fan audience. *SuperWhoLock* fan-page administrator Amy agrees with Ben (the Twelfth Doctor's "personality reminds [her] a lot of Sherlock") and notes that, with the premiere of Capaldi as the Twelfth Doctor, "I haven't seen as much new material for *SuperWhoLock* lately. I've seen a lot of stuff with the Eleventh Doctor, but since the Twelfth Doctor I haven't seen as much creation between the fandom's crossovers." (Although Capaldi-focused *SuperWhoLock* art exists.) She believes this is because it is "like that's having two of the same character" in *SuperWhoLock* texts, as Capaldi's Twelfth Doctor is similar to Cumberbatch's portrayal of Sherlock Holmes.

What is telling about these three texts is not just the interplay between the fan community, digital technology, and fannish innovation, but rather the multitudes of ways fans both ally and distance themselves from the text. Amy sees both similarities and differences between the various fan groups within *SuperWhoLock*. For her,

> the *Sherlock* fan community is very much like the *Supernatural* fan community. …They become a lot more active, like coming up with Meta, similar to how *Supernatural* does…*Doctor Who* is a lot more historical fandom, so it's hard to be involved that way. Because there's so much history and canon that goes into it. that I feel that it's a lot more difficult to be vested. …it doesn't feel like you're completely part of that fandom because there are still those pieces you're missing.

At the same time, another fan, Ben, noted that:

> *Doctor Who* and *Sherlock* fandoms are very respectful of each other …the fans seemed to—they seemed to be fans of both, or fans of one or the other and saying "I can respect what Sherlock's doing." It's a nice fandom to be involved with.

And for Vidalie:

> Every fandom is a community—with codes, with references, with cosplay, and thought. … That's the big difference between fandoms. It's where there's a [commonality] with the author, the same vision [between fan and creator].

Aja Romano writes that "though the [*SuperWhoLock*] trend was widespread [in Jan. 2012], it did not really pick up as a mass phenomenon until a few months later, perhaps in part because of a popular fictional trailer for the SuperWhoLockian universe … [which] has racked up over 13,000 reblogs since it was posted in April."[40] Although the video that Romano mentions has been taken down from YouTube, there are actually multiple other trailers that emerged at the same time that continue to garner views: one posted on 02 April 2012 by hath5712 titled "the lonely assassins trailer—superwholock" uses the Weeping Angels from *Doctor Who* as a villain against which Sherlock and the Winchesters must battle. It currently has over 30,000 views. Another video, posted a bit earlier on 29 March 2012 by Kanál uživatele TheMartyDee and titled "Superwholock—Don't Blink" also uses the Weeping Angels as a villain, but combines scenes of Dean Winchester and John Watson walking in the woods and talking to Sherlock on the phone. They encounter a Weeping Angel (a nice shot/reverse shot match as Watson uses a flashlight to look around and the video cuts to the Angel with a flashlight beam hitting it) and then ask the

Doctor (Tennant) to advise them via communication through a laptop. All this is remixed with the song "Lux Aeterna" by Clint Mansell from *Requiem for a Dream* and "Mortal Gladiator" by Focus Music, which lends a dramatic air to the fight between Castiel and Moriarty. The trailer ends with Moriarty accusing Sherlock of "being on the side of the Angels" as if to indicate betrayal among the heroes.[41] Romano concludes that:

> the creativity and ongoing popularity of this fandom meme seems to have its roots in the elements that made these shows popular to begin with. As *Supernatural*'s creator Eric Kripke points out, modern urban legends are "every bit as fleshed out as any world mythologies." We might say the same thing about the new legends that fandom creates for itself.[42]

And although she notes inklings of discontent in the different fan groups, the crossover phenomenon seems to be going strong. The emergence of *SuperWhoLock* in 2012 might seem like a flash-in-the-pan moment, a brief appearance of a kooky crossover. But as I write this three years later, *SuperWhoLock* continues as fan fiction, fan art, fan videos, and fan Gif Fics, and more emerged with the *Sherlock* New Year's special "The Abominable Bride."

What is perhaps one of the salient issues of *SuperWhoLock* is the role of gender in the construction of these alternate narratives. From the earliest days of fan studies, fan work (especially transformative fan work) has been linked to feminine styles of engagement with a media text. From Jenkins' and Bacon-Smith's germinal work on the female fan communities that shared fan fiction, and Penley's examination of female slash fans, to Busse's more contemporary look at the way gender influences interpretations of hierarchy within fan mainstreaming, the connections between fan groups and gendered media creation have been influential in the field.[43] *SuperWhoLock* is thus both notable for the vast female fandom that defines it—far more women than men create and share *SuperWhoLock* (on an already gendered social media technology like Tumblr) and the transformative properties of the crossover are themselves a highly gendered reading of the original texts. Notably, there is a strong female fan base for all three shows, although all three shows are also notable for the traditional masculinization and patriarchy contained within them—Steven Moffat is critiqued online for the sexism of *Doctor Who* and *Sherlock*,[44] while *Supernatural*'s rather tumultuous relationship with women has been well documented.[45] That female fans are therefore turning to alternate modes of expression and creation to develop new readings of these masculinized texts is unsurprising. By re-reading the masculine identities of the protagonists as more feminine, more in touch with feelings, emotions, and relationships, more open to alternative lifestyles, the texts of *SuperWhoLock* construct a deliberate and focused new take on traditional gendered ideas of narrative and story within cult media.

Engaging with the Fan-Brand of *SuperWhoLock*

Earlier, I defined *SuperWhoLock* as an example of "intra-transmediation," and, in this section, I want to describe what I mean by this by looking closely at the way the crossover fan text becomes a site of fan-branding. In using the term "brand," I am immediately problematizing *SuperWhoLock*, for it necessarily does not have *one* brand. Instead, I want to consider the fan experience of *SuperWhoLock* as a *fan-branded* experience, relying on Arvidsson's analysis of brands not just as corporate identifiers, but as "capitalist response[s] to the hypermediatization of the social that prevails in informational capitalism."[46] For Arvidsson, brands are social schemas that play an important role in our cultural identity: we identify ourselves by the brands we subscribe to, monetizing our affect and our experiences. The fan-brand of *SuperWhoLock* mirrors a particular dichotomy within these schemas, however: Arvidsson notes that just as brand initiatives create "intensive control" over user activity, so too can "strategies …aim at a high degree of universality …where user activity is difficult to steer."[47] Informational capitalism blurs the distinction between production, consumption, and circulation, and revisits the economic "value" of media texts in a digital age.

SuperWhoLock becomes an exemplar of this informational capitalism, as the fan-branded experience resides both outside all three texts and entirely within them. By branding, I refer not just to the specific distinguishing characteristics of each text (and of *SuperWhoLock* as a whole), but rather as a discourse that shapes the way fans socially understand the text(s) in context. For Matt Hills, fan-branding describes the process by which fans have "taken over" the production of *Doctor Who*, specifically, as a way of maintaining control over a franchise they love.[48] In contrast, I argue here that the fan-branding of *SuperWhoLock* is a way of looking at how fans themselves become (and create) their own brands within a divisive media landscape. Liz Moor argues that "branding *as a discourse*" emerged in the contemporary media era at the same time as brands have become engaged within fannish dialogue and work.[49] Celia Lury calls brands "objects" that organize and function as "a dynamic set of relationship between products."[50] It is in this sense, then, that I mean to situate *SuperWhoLock* as a particular fan-branding exercise.

For fans of *SuperWhoLock*, joining together the three texts becomes a sort of identifier; the characters and situations utilized in each *SuperWhoLock* story or image come from a corpus of elements and are reconstructed in new patterns that deliberately reflect the fans' preferences. According to David Banash, here writing about the practice of collecting objects, collecting is an inherently nostalgic practice: "to become a collector…is to engage profoundly with the past and the energies of nostalgia."[51] Collecting objects becomes a way of paying homage to what has come before and preserving the past. Yet, the mentalities of collecting vacillate between preservation and usage: we can collect and preserve objects, but in the digital age, we can more obvious collect ***and use*** digital artifacts without degradation. Banash calls this the "practice and the metaphor" of collecting—that consumption of the digital object mirrors the collecting of the physical.[52]

SuperWhoLock fandom manifests a similar interaction between preservation and utilization. Fans preserve narrative moments in their *SuperWhoLock* work but utilize them as a way of marking themselves as different from other fans. Rather than looking specifically at the brands developed within the text (e.g., the BBC, the CW), *SuperWhoLock* reflects a sense that fans are branding their own personal experience of fandom—that fandom becomes the "object" or "artifact" of the unique fannish experience.[53] Indeed, *SuperWhoLock* has no particular brand, except insofar as it resides within the (adopted) brands of the BBC and the CW. However, these media brands become important to the fan communities. Because they use footage from both channels, in many *SuperWhoLock* videos (including the video discussed above, hath5712's "the lonely assassins trailer—superwholock"), the logo for BBC One appears at the bottom of the screen throughout the video, even when clips from *Supernatural* display the show's network CW.

Although *SuperWhoLock* has never actually been branded, one fan, Johnslynn, sees the branding possibilities:

> seeing them come together even if it's just for one episode, I think that would be really cool. I just don't know how that would happen, because

> *Doctor Who* and *Sherlock* are on BBC and *Supernatural* is on CW. So I could see *Doctor Who* and *Sherlock* come together at some point, I just don't see how *Supernatural* would fit into that. But I think that would be really cool.

By constructing *SuperWhoLock* in particular ways, fans are situating their own fandom as a site of fan ritualization. Perhaps Sherlock and the Doctor are alike because they are high-functioning sociopaths? Perhaps Castiel and Watson are forever the sidekicks? Each *SuperWhoLock* text does not just tell the story of the protagonists, but tells the story of the fan.

The narrative existents of *Supernatural*, *Doctor Who*, and *Sherlock* are both mirrored in *SuperWhoLock* (they have to take on the characteristics of the original in order to reference back to the show) but also consumed (they have to react differently given the new narrative situations). This sort of intra-transmediation becomes the way a single text can take on characteristics of transmediation through the intra-textual connections held within the text. Transmedia storytelling, as defined by Henry Jenkins, describes "stories that unfold across multiple media platforms, with each medium making distinction contributions to our understanding of the world."[54] A transmediated world is spread out among multiple media outlets. Jenkins's quintessential example is *The Matrix*, as the multiple films, video games, Manga titles, anime, and DVD releases all construct an uber-narrative that detailed the entire world. Importantly, transmediation is also a corporate operation: each entity within the franchise becomes another form of marketing. As Kozinets argues, today's "business managers, strategists, and particularly marketers have hit upon the notion that consumers should be courted as more than mere consumers; they need to become 'fans'."[55] By creating transmedia franchises, media corporations interpellate fan practices as normative. Today, the media landscape is not only embracing transmediation, but also becoming itself more transmediated. As fans (and audiences generally) can follow multiple threads through a media universe, that universe itself (rather than the texts individually) seems more transmediated.

In *Digital Fandom*, I described the concept of "intra-textuality" as the mechanism by which "meaning … occurs inside the document text itself." In other words, "whereas intertextuality exists *in-between* texts, intra-textuality implies *movement within a whole*" and "is a useful tool for investigating narratives that cross technologies of distribution channels.[56] Intra-textuality helps illustrate the ways that transmediated texts are different from non-transmediated texts, as the connective tissues that guide fans' understanding of media texts cohere in strongly bonded ties.

SuperWhoLock offers a useful study of a text that is seemingly transmediated, but is not. The three separate texts that construct *SuperWhoLock* are combined into one media channel. Because there is no official "canon" of *SuperWhoLock*, there is also no authoritative source against which fans can compare their creation—which in effect makes every *SuperWhoLock* text an "official" *SuperWhoLock* text. In addition, there is no canon toward which fans can intra-textually see the transmedial connections. Since *Supernatural*, *Doctor Who*, and *Sherlock* are themselves separate texts with separate universes, they do not create a transmediated text on their own—only with the fannish intra-transmediation, do the three texts become one.

SuperWhoLock, as its own universe that makes use of the disparate universes of the original text, is not transmediated either but gives the appearance of a transmediated text through its aesthetic sensibilities. Any particular instantiation of *SuperWhoLock* will necessarily only give a slice of the larger world, hinting at events or adventures that have not happened. For example, in Fig. 1.7, artist oyo has posited Watson and Sherlock debating a Dalek while the Doctor eats fish fingers and custard. This image raises far more questions than it answers, and hints at far larger narrative issues than can possibly be answered in any fictionalized canon—why is there a

Fig. 1.7 *Doctor Who* at Baker Street, by oyo (http://oooyooo.tumblr.com/post/16374389449/sherlock-arguing-with-a-dalek-could-anybody)

Dalek and why is it not exterminating people? What are they debating? Where are the Doctor's companions? Is the Dalek the companion?

The hints and possibilities hearken to a type of transmedia engagement with a main text; as if what we are seeing here is just one part of a much larger series. Engaging with this sort of textual questioning lies at the heart of *SuperWhoLock* as it embraces the intra-transmediated characteristics of the crossover. Only by seeing these three requisite texts as separate can meaning be constructed: fans have to read the Dalek in a manner consistent with the Daleks in *Doctor Who* in order to understand the relationship in Fig. 1.7. But by necessity, such reading undermines the separation of the three texts because they come together as one, cohered into a type of mashup.[57]

SuperWhoLock thus becomes a site of fan meaning-construction and in many ways is applicable to the way fans engage in trans-fandom discussions at fan conventions. Although many conventions may seem traditionally uni-fandom (e.g., focused only on *Doctor Who*), in fact, they are often built on dissecting the relationships between multiple texts. Fan conventions are like memory palaces, argues Nicolle Lamerichs, that "although public, relies on private meaning and past experiences… [It] is not a historical site but a constructed one in which the place is arranged to have connections to fiction."[58] *SuperWhoLock*, similarly, is like a fan convention in that it is a site constructed from the interior meanings fans give to the requisite texts and the trans-fandom between them. One fans' experiences with *Supernatural*, *Doctor Who*, and *Sherlock* may be vastly different than another's, but in that difference lies the actualization of the *SuperWhoLock* fan text. In the digital age, the experience of being a fan has changed. Yet, as Peter Kelly and I have shown:

> many aspects of fan identity have remained relatively unchanged, despite the rapid diffusion of new technology into fans' lives. In fact, with little exception, much of what was written about fans twenty-five years ago applies just as well today. Yet, although fandom has not been revolutionized, it also does not entirely resemble the community of twenty-five years ago, nor do fans exactly channel fans of years past.[59]

SuperWhoLock is a way of marking particular episodes in the fan experience—resonate moments of *Supernatural*, *Doctor Who*, and *Sherlock* that create a particular fan-brand. Even if the fannish experience is similar to the past—perhaps because it is—fans are creating their own unique fandoms to differentiate themselves from the past. *SuperWhoLock* is this differentiation.

According to Cornel Sandvoss, fans control the narrative universe of their particular texts by their "shaping of textual boundaries." He argues "popular texts thus function as spaces of self-reflection, not only through the individual interpretation of particular signs, but also through a selective process of which signs are part of the fan text in the first place."[60] I do not mean to argue here that one can supposedly "see into the soul" of fan by looking at the *SuperWhoLock* texts she puts together. Such psychological correspondence simplifies the relationship here, and is ultimately reductive. What I do want to argue, though, is that *SuperWhoLock* takes mundane moments from the text—a small glance here, a smile there—and elevates them into meaningful fan discourse. *SuperWhoLock* becomes a site of fan productivity which "relies on creating a longing for lost objects that never actually came to pass."[61] In a similar analysis, Godwin looks at fans who take existing action figures and re-sculpt them into new forms, to customize them to reflect different textual attributes or non-sanctioned uses. Fans are making something new that reflects unique aspects of the fan experience. For Godwin, these modified action figures provide "a useful resource to address intersections of multi-dimensional fandom."[62] As an aspect of trans-fandom, *SuperWhoLock* helps researchers explore the boundaries of these fan dimensions, developing workable analyses of when a fandom morphs into a trans-fandom.

Chapter Summary

Each chapter in this book relates the fan audience for the particular requisite text to *SuperWhoLock* through interview research at fan conventions. It is not my intent to artificially separate out the fans for these shows—that is, most of the fans I spoke with would consider themselves "trans-fans" who see their fannishness reflected for multiple texts at once. But by exploring each of these fans in their own convention space, I hope to contrast the different ways the media industries explore and market fandom to fans as disparate. Mirroring the way that individuals "get into" *SuperWhoLock* (e.g., becoming a fan of one or two shows and then finding the phenomenon online), chapters can be read in any order.

The second chapter offers a discussion and critique of the corporate ownership of fandom through the metaphor of the Creation *Supernatural* con as it relates to larger fan convention culture.[63] I will discuss and analyze the specific politics of what I call "fanqueue" culture, or a culture of sanctioned consumerism as cultural capital. Fanqueue culture is defined by the eagerness to wait in lines, or what Zubernis and Larsen describe as the way fans "can buy proximity" to the guests.[64] Fans are both reliant on and influence the larger corporate culture guiding fandom. Creation Entertainment represents the resistant/complicit state of fandom within the industry, and serves to understand the mainstreaming of fan audiences in the digital age.

In the third chapter, I tie the notion of "affective play" to the hierarchies and power relations at *Gallifrey One*, a contemporary *Doctor Who* fan convention.[65] In contrast to the *Supernatural* fan convention, where fan-created events happen outside the boundaries of Creation's plan, at the *Doctor Who* fan convention, fan-events dominate. At the same time, specific fan markers present ruptures in this homogenous identity; the rise of "ribbon culture" heralds a key turn in fan power relations. Fans affix numerous ribbons to their badges, and eventually each fan may have a unique rainbow of ribbons cascading down their front (some fans' ribbons are so long, they trail on the floor). Such ribbons become a playful aspect of the fan convention, but also affix a measure of power to the intra-fan relationship. In this way, Gallifrey One becomes a convention residing within the tension of capitalism and gift, as a new form of what I have previously defined as the Digi-gratis economy.[66]

In the fourth chapter, I expand on the role of expertise in fan communities by analyzing the Sherlocked fan convention held in London in April 2015. The Sherlocked convention was run by Massive Events and Showmasters, which, like Creation, are for-profit, corporate entities, in partnership with Handmade Films, the company that produces *Sherlock*. In line with the corporatization of fan practices, Massive Events instituted a highly stratified pricing strategy for the event: the cheapest option for attending the complete convention was £45, the most expensive scheme was £2995. The fan response to Sherlocked tells of a classism within fandom, and speaks to the way *SuperWhoLock* creates a new form of textuality that seems to exceed traditional notions of fan economics. In fan communities, there was an uproar when the pricing was announced, as nearly £3000 for a convention seems to price out many who might want to attend. In response, then, fans organized their own Unlocked convention to occur on Tumblr. This Unlocked convention featured free panels, simultaneous screenings, and chats in contrast to pricy Sherlocked event.

The conclusion to the book brings *SuperWhoLock* back together to examine the nature of the multiple allegiances of *SuperWhoLock* fans. Rarely is one a fan of *SuperWhoLock* without some familiarity and fandom of at least one of the other texts. But because of the unique inter-fandom transmediation of *SuperWhoLock*, this leads to fan antagonism between fans with multiple interpretations of the text(s) at the heart of the corpus.[67] While much *SuperWhoLock* work explores the connections between texts (and the majority of this book looks at connections between fans), there are still antagonistic and anti-fan sentiments among the *Supernatural*, *Doctor Who*, and *Sherlock* fan communities. The conclusion explores these antagonisms as a meaningful element within *SuperWhoLock*'s text. Indeed, just as fan fiction is a "work in progress," so too are fan groups continually in the process of creating and adjusting boundaries between fan objects and hierarchies between fans.[68] In this analysis, therefore, I hope to get a more well-rounded and generative portrait of the digital fan audience.

Notes

1. Byrne-Cristiano, "BBC and CW."
2. Perez, "GIF Fics."
3. Harvey, "Sherlock's Webs," 119.
4. Steward, "Homes in the Small Screen," 133.
5. Stein and Busse, "Introduction," 18.
6. Hills, "Fandom as an Object," 158–9; see Booth, "Reifying the Fan"; Hills, "Doctor Who's Travels"; Hills, "Patterns of Surprise."
7. Scott, "Who's Steering the Mothership?"
8. Stein, *Millennial Fandom*; Watley, "Race, Gender, and Digital Media."
9. Booth, *Playing Fans.*
10. Booth, *Playing Fans*; Busse, "Geek Hierarchies"; Hills, "Torchwood's Trans-Transmedia"; Jenkins, "Afterword"; Pullen, "*The Lord of the Rings.*"
11. Hills, "'Twilight' Fans."
12. Booth, "Reifying the Fan," 147.
13. Jenkins, *Textual Poachers*; Booth, "Rereading Fandom."
14. Booth, *Time on TV.*
15. Busse and Hellekson, "Introduction."
16. Booth, *Digital Fandom.*
17. Coppa, "Fuck Yeah," 80.
18. Hills, *Fan Cultures*; Sandvoss, *Fans.*
19. Hills, "Recognition in the Eyes"; Geraghty, *Living with Star Trek.*

20. Booth, "Reifying the Fan"; Booth, *Playing Fans.*
21. Pearson, "Fandom."
22. Booth, "*BioShock.*"
23. Jenkins, "Afterword"; Jenkins, "Transmedia 202"; Booth, *Digital Fandom*, 55–78.
24. Booth, *Playing Fans.*
25. Geraghty, *Cult Collectors*; Zubernis and Larsen, *Fandom at the Crossroads.*
26. Zubernis and Larsen, *Fandom at the Crossroads.*
27. Although, see Bacon-Smith, *Enterprising Women*; Zubernis and Larsen, *Fandom at the Crossroads*; Geraghty, *Cult Collectors*; Lamerichs, "Stranger Than Fiction"; Lamerichs, "Embodied Fantasy."
28. Perez, "Gif Fics," 149.
29. Not her real name.
30. https://www.facebook.com/superwholockiansunited?fref=ts.
31. Perez, "Gif Fics"; Booth, *Playing Fans.*
32. Marshall, "Animated GIFs"; Uhlin, "Playing."
33. Booth, *Playing Fans*, 26.
34. Email correspondence 11 March 2015.
35. Email correspondence 11 March 2015.
36. Morris, "Britain as Fantasy"; Lausch, "The Niche Network."
37. Harrigan and Wardrip-Fruin, "Introduction"; Britton, *TARDISBound*; Perryman, "*Doctor Who.*"
38. Perez, "Gif Fics," 150.
39. Perez, "Gif Fics," 155.
40. Romano, "WTF."
41. https://www.youtube.com/watch?v=ydq0u3A-QlE.
42. Romano, "WTF."
43. Jenkins, *Textual Poachers*; Bacon-Smith, *Enterprising Women*; Penley, "Feminism"; Busse, "Geek Hierarchies."
44. See Romano, "Why Does and Man?"
45. See the fourth issue of *Transformative Works and Cultures.*
46. Arvidsson, *Brands*, 136.
47. Arvidsson, *Brands*, 121.
48. Hills, *Triumph of a Time Lord.*
49. Moor, *The Rise of Brands*, 5.
50. Lury, *Brands*, 48.
51. Banash, "Virtual Life," 63.
52. Banash, "Virtual Life," 56.
53. Lury, *Brands*, 49.
54. Jenkins, *Convergence Culture*, 293.
55. Kozinets, "Fan Creep," 162.
56. Booth, *Digital Fandom*, 6–7, 56–8.

57. Gunkel, "Rethinking the Digital Remix," 489.
58. Lamerichs, "Embodied Fantasy," 268, cited in Hills, *Unfolding Event*, 70.
59. Booth and Kelly, "Changing Faces," 57.
60. Sandvoss, *Fans*, 132.
61. Church, *Grindhouse Nostalgia*, 139, cited in Hills, *Unfolding Event*, 34.
62. Godwin, "G.I. Joe Vs. Barbie," 122.
63. Booth, *Playing Fans*.
64. Zubernis and Larsen, *Fandom at the Crossroads*, 25.
65. Hills, *Fan Cultures*; see Booth and Kelly, "Changing Faces" for an analysis of a different convention, Chicago TARDIS.
66. Booth, *Digital Fandom*, 24.
67. Karkanias, "Dynamics of Fandom."
68. Busse and Hellekson, "Introduction."

CHAPTER 2

Supernatural Fandom: The Fandom Business

Abstract This chapter discusses and critiques the corporate ownership of fan conventions through a discussion of Creation Entertainment's *Supernatural* convention. It introduces the concept of "fanqueue" culture, defined as fans' sanctioned consumerism. Tying this to *SuperWhoLock*, the chapter explores a tension in fandom between fan readings and corporate readings of fan cultures. That is, fans both are reliant upon and influence the larger corporate culture guiding fandom. The chapter argues that, although such Creation Entertainment may not encourage fan spaces, fans create their own spaces at Creation, just as they do with *SuperWhoLock*, and thus preserve the unique moments of their own fan identity.

Keywords *Supernatural* • Fanqueue • Tiering • Conference • Creation Entertainment • Affirmational fandom

SuperWhoLock fandom, as what I have called an intra-transmediated fandom, does more than just tie three texts together; *SuperWhoLock* also bridges some of the different fan *groups* that cluster around their objects of fandom. Fandom is not a homogenous space, but rather a cluster of interactive and interacting groups, with individuals moving from text to text with what Hills has described as a "trans-fandom" affective experience.[1] *SuperWhoLock* manifests this interaction as a subcultural text that may or

P. Booth, *Crossing Fandoms*, DOI 10.1057/978-1-137-57455-8_2

may not be accepted within all fan communities. But what do different fan communities make of the phenomenon—and how can we understand how fandom itself manifests in different groups, at different times, and in different spaces?

This chapter discusses and critiques the corporate manifestation of fandom at the Creation *Supernatural* convention.[2] I will discuss and analyze the specific characteristics of what I am calling "fanqueue" culture, or a culture of sanctioned consumerism as cultural capital. Fanqueue culture is defined by the eagerness to wait in lines, or what Zubernis and Larsen describe as the way fans "can buy proximity" to the guests at a convention.[3] Creation's *Supernatural* convention features no discussion panels and just one main stage, where actors (and very occasionally behind-the-scenes personnel) entertain the crowd with music, dancing, standup comedy, and answering questions. Almost everything at Creation conventions involves waiting in lines. At the same time, the main stage speakers serve an important regulatory function—that is, the majority of the stage banter both reinforces the hierarchies present within the authorized convention space and concretizes the centralizing authority of the two stars of the show, Jared Padalecki (who plays Sam Winchester) and Jensen Ackles (who plays his brother Dean Winchester). As the first discussion in a larger analysis of *SuperWhoLock* as a metaphor for contemporary fandom, then, this chapter will focus on the affirmational and celebratory aspects of the tripartite text. Creation Entertainment serves a useful purpose for fans and media institutions in an era of fan mainstreaming, and offers an heuristic against which we can compare the way other fan conventions function.

More so than the discussion of "consumerism and resistance"—where fans are seen to be both consumers of cultural products and resistant to the underlying ideological messages of those texts—the discourses about the influence and commodification of fans in *Supernatural* fandom highlights the way Creation Entertainment manages and discursively constructs fan activities into commercial realms.[4] That Creation is a "well-oiled" machine, as Karen, one of my interviewees, noted, helps to naturalize this convention style for fans—the convention reifies the stage show as a symbol of the television series *Supernatural* itself, the central nexus around which fans congregate. As I will demonstrate, this nexus creates an "affirmational bubble" in the convention space which normalizes the experience of fans as consumers.

By emphasizing the centrality of the text within the fandom, Creation largely reifies the fan-as-consumer practice of fandom. Fans at the con are normalized into this role through aspects like tiered pricing, fanqueue culture, and affirmational attendance. In this way, Creation's *Supernatural* convention provides a foil for the type of creative fan exploration represented by *SuperWhoLock*. I have previously argued that "although *SuperWhoLock* ... [is] fan created, [it relies] on an understanding of the dominant messages of the original texts." In other words, *SuperWhoLock* lies at the heart of a nexus of multiple tensions, a "number of ambiguous relationships: between fan fiction and fan vidding, between masculine and feminine discursive styles of fandom, between affirmational and transformative fandom. [*SuperWhoLock* embodies] multiplicity and thus [is] indicative of larger paradigms of discursive ambiguity within fandom as well."[5] These tensions also emerge in fans' convention culture.

Fans are anonymous at Creation conventions. No name tags are worn (although lanyards are provided as a "perk" of upgrading to a more expensive ticket), and fans are instead constructed by the physical and social space of the convention as a relatively amorphous but hierarchized mass. Importantly, many fans at the convention readily accept this traditionally fannish identity as given, and—I stress this—heartily enjoy being a consumer (as opposed to being a cultural resistor). In the special issue of *Transformative Works and Cultures* devoted to *Supernatural* fandom, Laura Felschow argues that Creation Entertainment's conventions "are useful illustrations of the kind of fan loyalty ... that *Supernatural* has created."[6] My ultimate aim in this chapter is to establish why Creation's model is so successful in a world where fan studies argues the cultural resistance of fans.

Although Creation's model of programming may not deliberately encourage fan spaces, they do create areas for fans to replicate a resistant interpretation. Fans create their own spaces at Creation—as with *SuperWhoLock*—and thus preserve the unique moments of their own fan identity. Interestingly, of the multiple conventions I attended to interview fans, the fans that attended this Creation convention were singular in their view of the convention experience. Whereas the fans at Gallifrey One or the Sherlocked convention shared many differing opinions about their experiences at conventions and how they felt how conventions should be run, the fans at the *Supernatural* con almost universally agreed that they preferred Creation's style of convention over any other—most interviewees compared it to the massive San Diego Comic-Con. That there might be an alternate to this sort of corporate conventions did not seem to occur to the fans I spoke with, revealing the way that Creation dominates the conceptualization of the convention for these fans. What Creation actually creates is a tension for the fan between enjoying and accepting his/her consumerist position at the con while maintaining an awareness that he/she is being forced to accept that position.

Importantly, I want to structure this argument around the existence and metaphor of *SuperWhoLock*. Just as the nature of *SuperWhoLock* is as a three-part combination of disjointed texts, whose meaning arrives in the spaces in-between the texts, so too does the *Supernatural* convention (and the fans at it) give meaning to the other conventions by the lacuna between each fan space. The establishment of the fandom-created *SuperWhoLock*, a text that fan Colleen argues "just [has] such a rabid fan base that … like these things so much. So there's as much crossover as they can get" provides a heuristic for understanding the construction of the fan in this era of mainstreaming.

After discussing the role of *Supernatural* within *SuperWhoLock*, I turn to an analysis of Creation conventions as an affirmational fan performance. The term "affirmational fandom" comes from an influential blog post by fan obsession_inc, who argues that there are largely two types of fan works—affirmational fandom, which views the text as central and "affirms" the canon and creator, and transformational fandom, which views the text as one iteration among many and "transforms" its boundaries via fan fiction, vidding, and art.[7] Although this model has been critiqued by Matt Hills, it remains a useful model for analyzing different types of fan creations—not in a reductive "either/or" binary but rather on a continuum spanning affirmational and transformational.[8] Creation's *Supernatural* con skews heavily toward the affirmational, but fans at the con, like the fans that create *SuperWhoLock*, employ strategies to contest this ambiguity. (In the next chapter, I will examine Gallifrey One, a *Doctor Who* convention, that skews more toward the transformational.) Ultimately, *SuperWhoLock* provides a useful heuristic for understanding the complex role that consumerism and affirmational fan activities play in an ever-changing transformative fan environment.

SuperWhoLock: Progress in Works

Supernatural tells the story of the Winchester brothers—Sam and Dean—who are in the "Family Business" of hunting monsters, demons, and other supernatural evil. The show has morphed since it first started, illustrating a flexibility within its genre. What started as a horror-themed show on the now-failed WB network in 2005 has become (as of 2015) 11 seasons of family drama with supernatural monsters shown on the CW network for an audience of highly energized fans. As aca-fans Katherine Larsen and Lynn Zubernis describe, *Supernatural* is multilayered, with "sibling rivalry, unresolved oedipal drama, reluctant heroes. A story of family ties, love, and loyalty. An emotionally intense relationship between the two main characters that generates enough chemistry to power a small city."[9]

In many ways, then, *Supernatural* fits easily into the *SuperWhoLock* (non)diegesis. Like *Doctor Who* and *Sherlock*, it features attractive protagonists who fight against evil, it plays on and with emotional angst, and it focuses on disaffected (or anti-social and odd) characters who just do not fit into the world around them. Just as *Supernatural* (as well as *Doctor Who* and, to a lesser extent, *Sherlock*) has changed over time, so too does *SuperWhoLock*: as Amy noted, "The narrative for *SuperWhoLock* changes based on what is current in the shows and it is always adapting. Everyone has their own version of a crossover narrative and I think it makes for a brilliant creative pool of ideas." But as with the other two ingredients for this cultish potpourri, *Supernatural* also does not *quite* fit. Unlike *Doctor Who* and *Sherlock*, *Supernatural* is American, has no particular long history (although its focus on mythology and urban legends does have antecedents into the past), and has few sci-fi elements. Thus, just as the other two texts find themselves sitting uneasily within this crossover, *Supernatural* is both a part of and apart from the idea of *SuperWhoLock* itself. This type of inter- and intra-textual significance can be seen in, for example, Fig. 2.1, a rendition of *SuperWhoLock* by artist Nupao found on DeviantArt.

In this image, all three texts are represented as disparate but connected; *Supernatural* in the middle is flanked by *Sherlock* on the left and *Doctor Who* on the right. Additionally, the main characters from each of these shows—John Watson, Sherlock Holmes, Crowley, Dean and Sam Winchester, Castiel, and the Tenth and Eleventh Doctors—are back-

Fig. 2.1 *SuperWhoLock*, by Nupao (http://www.deviantart.com/art/Superwholock-292182438)

grounded in comparison to three major villains from each of these series—Moriarty, Lucifer, and the Master—each of whom is in the foreground of the image. The image is in triptych style, with heavy purple lines trisecting the image and creating separate compartments for each of the shows. In this way, a separation between the protagonists is emphasized (e.g., Sherlock's body and Dean Winchester's body do not overlap) while the antagonists form a single cohesive group. The aesthetics of the image—both cartoonish but also realistic—also emphasize a duality within the *SuperWhoLock* text between reliance on the actual (the canon text) and the virtual (the fan-created mashup of the three).[10] Interestingly, Nupao has also created a commissioned genderbent version of this image, wherein all the characters' sexes have been switched from male to female and an extra character (presumably the person for whom the genderbent image was created) has been added to the *Doctor Who* portion.[11] While genderbending, as Ann McClellan states, "contributes to the ways we theorize about sex and gender and simultaneously risks reinforcing and potentially limiting common cultural understandings of the differences between the two concepts," it also can serve as a metaphor for understanding the way fans respond to traditional representations of characters.[12] In many ways, the characters within *SuperWhoLock* narratives, while remaining the same sex as in their original, perform a similar function as do the genderbent versions: as both problematically part of a patriarchal media system but also as autonomous entities with sexed characteristics. For artist Nupao, genderbending serves as another tool through which *SuperWhoLock* can reveal discourses and discords between these three texts.

At the same time, Nupao's image highlights another aspect of *SuperWhoLock* that reflects the way the unique fan-brand of the mashup emerges in the fandom environment—the emphasis on character as a central motif. With no centralized text upon which to base the *SuperWhoLock* fan works, fans must engage with the characters of the shows to develop an understanding of how they might function together. For example, fan mikedimayuga explores what might happen were the protagonists from the three shows to meet at a bar (all sic):

> 1—dean and sherlock would dislike each other in their first meeting. i figure they're both alpha dogs [...] i'm sure by the end they will have some grudging mutual respect....
>
> 2—sam and watson would be instant best friends, having so much in common. they would trade war stories and complain about their partners.
>
> 3—[the] doc[tor] would be fascinated with castiel. [...] it would be gloriously awkward.[13]

Analyzing these comments critically, we can see that the connections between the characters become the most important focus of *SuperWhoLock*.

For the *Supernatural* aspect of *SuperWhoLock*, there are really three characters that emerge as the most consistently popular: the two sibling protagonists Sam and Dean Winchester and their erstwhile colleague Castiel, an Angel. Dean is most often portrayed as argumentative and disbelieving (he rarely understands why the TARDIS is bigger on the inside) while Sam is more talkative and earnest. Castiel is most often depicted as confused and irritated by human technology and idiosyncrasies. The Doctor is just as curious and flummoxed by humans as Castiel is; Sherlock is just as anti-social as Dean; Watson is just as easy-going as Sam. For mikedimayuga, it is not just that one text might feature these characters, but that these characters might represent some tropes and characteristics in a larger sense than just a single show. *Supernatural* fan Johnslynn (her cosplay name) notes that much *SuperWhoLock* rests on "just different impersonation of the characters incorporated into one." The characters were central and overlook any narrative or diegetic issues between the shows.

The way the three shows' characters interact with one another was also highlighted by some of the fans, vendors, and convention personnel I spoke to at the Creation Entertainment *Supernatural* convention in Chicago, although fewer people at this convention were enthralled by *SuperWhoLock* than at other conventions I visited (see Chaps. 3 and 4). For instance, Colleen admitted that:

> realistically, [*SuperWhoLock* is] the silliest thing ever ... But it would be fun. I do really like all the fan work that people create with that... I think the fan stuff is really great for that—they don't have the restrictions of, the studios saying we can't [narratively] go in that direction, and blah blah all that—they just come up with whatever they think.

Fans conceptualize the way the characters interact with one another; *SuperWhoLock* is a fan mashup built from its characters rather than any particular story.

Key to understanding the fan group lies in the construction of difference between texts within *SuperWhoLock*. Interestingly, while most of the *Supernatural* fans I spoke with were both knowledgeable and interested in *SuperWhoLock*, the majority also saw *Sherlock* (of all the texts that construct *SuperWhoLock*) as the odd show out. What is perhaps most telling is how the fans are defining "difference" here. *Sherlock* is only unlike *Supernatural* in particular ways: most obviously, the genre is more based in realism, and the setting is in the UK rather than the USA. The fan base seems to define the importance of *Supernatural*, then, on its location and its genre characteristics. Karen noted that all three shows have "got similar vibes. ... I do not know if you can say that about *Sherlock*, but *Doctor Who* and *Supernatural* can be serious and then do not take themselves too seriously. I do not know if you can say that about *Sherlock*." Colleen said that "*Sherlock* ...is weird, because it has nothing to do with Sci-Fi." Lindsey noted that "They're all very similar. [But] *Sherlock* is not like *Supernatural*." It makes sense that the fans at a particular convention would see their text as central, and then the other text that is the "most different" as being the odd one out. (For instance, *Doctor Who* fans at *Gallifrey One* thought that *Supernatural* was quite the odd one out.)

There are, of course, other ways these differences could be defined: both *Sherlock* and *Supernatural* feature two handsome male protagonists (compare to *Doctor Who*, which only has one). Erik described this difference between the shows as "all three of the shows [feature] these guys that are just sort of roguish." Looked alternately still, another difference could be the way that in *Supernatural* and *Doctor Who,* the protagonists travel, while in *Sherlock,* they stay rooted at 221B Baker Street in London. Neither of these, however, seemed to crop up in our discussions of what made *Supernatural* different from *Sherlock.*

In other words, *SuperWhoLock* is constructed by *some* fans, for *some* fans; and as such, it is literally built to appeal to *particular* fan audiences. And unless you are not a fan in the same way that others practice their fandom, you run the risk of being alienated from the *SuperWhoLock* fandoms. Amy sees *SuperWhoLock* as the combination not of the three texts, but of the three fandoms: "While they might have been fans of one or the other…I think *SuperWhoLock* as a whole got pulled into the *Supernatural* fandom." One of the vendors at the *Supernatural* convention, Ginia, "sell[s] out all of [the *SuperWhoLock* merchandise] very quickly. … I do sell out of them faster than just my other fandom things." If there is a popularity for the mashup, it is based in the fandom itself, and it is to this fandom at the *Supernatural* convention that I next turn.

Creation Entertainment and *Supernatural* Fandom

Creation Entertainment, as a corporate entity, has structured *Supernatural* fan conventions as a site of affirmational fandom and creator's authority. Fan conventions have become one of the most centralized aspects of formal (mainstream) fandom in today's fannish media ecology and, as such, Creation's remit to focus on celebrities and authorized readings of the media program foregrounds a devotion to the original text at the expense of unauthorized fan activity, an emphasis which seemingly denies *SuperWhoLock*. However, it is non-affirmational fan work that tends to be analyzed more often in fan literature: as Hills questions, "Fan practices have often been approached as transformative, but what of fan communities that may not fit so readily or tidily into this bracket?"[14] Recognizing the affirmational fan community within the *Supernatural* convention space not only reflects *SuperWhoLock*'s "interactive potential" between "fans' affective appreciation of a text and their appropriation (and transformation) of the text,"[15] but also reveals a crucial aspect of today's mainstreamed fan audience.[16] That is, for *SuperWhoLock*, as with for any fan-created text, there must be some aspect of affirmational appreciation that resists transformational potential, and while *Supernatural* itself invites much transformational work (see, for example, Wincest, Manip, and Mpreg fic[17]), the authorized appreciation for the show and its actors manifests most directly at the Creation convention.

There have always been different types of fan conventions, appealing to different types of fan audiences. Lincoln Geraghty offers the convention space as "the primary location of mass fan gatherings for over 70 years," tracing fan conventions back to 1939's first World Science Fiction Convention in New York.[18] Many of the fans I spoke with at the *Supernatural* convention had been to other conventions, not just Creation ones, and they remarked that older conventions were hardly ever focused on actors, autographs, or purchasing items. Karen, for instance, had been to some of the earliest *Star Trek* conventions, where "there were probably twenty-five, maybe thirty of us. That's all it was. … there were no stars there or anything, we just watched copies of the pilot and bloopers." Mary did not have the resources to go to the types of *Star Trek* conventions that Karen did, but she was able to attend a *Dungeons & Dragons* convention in the 1970s. And when Jennifer R. was growing up, she felt like she "never had any hope of meeting" her idols. Today, she says, "people actually get a chance to meet the actors they really admire, look up to, have a crush on, whatever… you see the people that do this [at the] convention." Conventions have become one of the most popular ways of participating in fandom, and when I asked Karen (who has been going to conventions for over 40 years) why they have become such a major part of fandom today, she remarked that:

> Going to the [convention], which was twenty minutes away by interstate, was a big deal then. …And now there are people who can afford to travel much more maybe than they could back then, and were more inclined to travel from more rural places…I think it's evolved because people are more likely to travel now.

Jennifer argued that as fans have grown up, and have more disposable income and time, "we can do things we want to do. … We're enjoying the fact it's for us—but we want to experience it because I didn't get a chance to experience it [when I was younger]." Certainly, travel is easier today than in the past, and conventions have increasingly developed as sites of celebrity spotting.

Different fan conventions create different fan spaces. Today, some conventions are strictly fan-run: Zubernis and Larsen write about attending Wincon, the Winchester Writers Convention. At this con, "there were no celebrity guests, no photo ops, no autograph sessions, no actor Q&A's." Instead, it was a fan convention for and by fans—"it was like our online fandom," they write, "had been magically brought to life in the real world, without a shred of shame."[19] In an interview with the editors of *Transformative Works and Cultures*, Wincon organizer Ethrosdemon describes it as:

> by the fans, for the fans operation. Our goal is to provide an annual gathering for SPN fans ...to come and meet, hang out, discuss the show and the fic written about it, party and have a good time. ... No one from the show is affiliated with this convention, nor will there be any appearances by any show actors, writers, or other personnel.

Ethrosdemon goes on to describe Wincon's purpose as being:

> all about *us*, not about the actors or the show's creators. People come to Wincon to hang out in a comfortable environment with other people who are interested in similar media sources. .... A con like ours is a completely different beast from an actor con. Both serve their own purposes, and I don't think there is any competition between them, honestly. There is some crossover between the people who attend the cons, but even those people who do both will tell you frankly that the purposes are at wide variance. Actor cons offer access and a certain kind of insider trafficking that fan cons do not.[20]

Contrast Wincon with the most popular (literally in terms of population) "industry conventions" today, massive Comic-Cons like San Diego Comic-Con (SDCC), the Wizard World, Inc. run Wizard World conventions (currently 22 conventions a year), or ReedPop's massive conventions like Chicago's C2E2, New York's New York Comic Con, or Seattle's Emerald City Comicon.[21] These conventions, often sporting attendance numbering in the tens if not hundreds of thousands, are general "fan" cons with scores of media and entertainment guests, a focus on the dealer's room (i.e., consumptive practices[22]), and multiple speaker panels running simultaneously (some with fan speakers and others with industry/actor speakers). These more general conventions do not necessarily focus on one particular media text, but highlight instead the experience of fandom as filtered through a corporate body—a tension that reflects the "nomadic" experience of fans in today's hypermediated world.[23]

There are hundreds of conventions that fit somewhere in-between these two extremes. Conventions spaces thus allow multiple points of connection, what Geraghty summarizes as "emotional connections between fans and actors and between fans and fans, [as well as]...a space where commodities such as toys, props, and autographs could be bought and sold."[24] These spaces, however, are always mediated by external entities, a situation where the "social space[s]" between actors and fans.

> remains separate. Performers are protected (sometimes by convention staff and sometimes by bodyguards hired for the event) and kept in separate spaces (taking back routes through the hotels in which most conventions are held in order to avoid fan crowded hallways and lobbies) until they are presented to the fans under highly ritualized conditions.[25]

For Jennifer R., however, this mediated space is shrinking. Her (and her daughter's) experience reflects a simulacra of closeness with the celebrity:

> These guys [are] so friendly and they go out of their way. Like last year we walked up to Mark Sheppard for his autograph and [my daughter] was so nervous she couldn't say anything—she put her paper down, he signed it, and she was ready to run away and he's like, wait a minute, where are you from? And just so friendly. And they're all the same—Jensen, and Osric Chau, etc. She went to get her picture with Jared and Jensen, and they hugged her—you could just tell that they were like, you're among friends. So I thought that made it worth it, personally. I mean you're spending all this money, but it's what she really wanted. It's really worth it because the actors seem to be really interested in the fans.

Does a perception of interest indicate actual interest or not? For the fans at the *Supernatural* con, the answer seems to be that it does not matter.

The Affirmational Fan at the Convention

When asked about what makes Creation Entertainment different from other conventions, Adam Malin, co-founder and co-owner of the organization said:

> First of all, our profuse respect for intellectual property and the compelling need to license it and not utilize it without very specific permission from the creators, from the license holders.... Licensing was really key because, as a creator myself I have a strong respect for content ownership, intellectual property ownership. .... Most conventions, and virtually all the fan conventions in the marketplace are not licensed, and there is actually some flagrant abuse of intellectual property rights. And that's something that we have a real problem with.

The licensing of the entertainment property takes many forms. At Creation's *Supernatural* convention, for instance, there were very few vendors selling fan-created works (e.g., artwork). There were some, such as Ginia, who sold scarves with *SuperWhoLock* patterns on them, but no artists or unauthorized dealers. In addition, the entire Creation Entertainment philosophy of the convention is structured around one main stage event, with the consequence of focusing entirely on the participation of the actors. In contrast to other conventions, which often feature multiple discussion panels running at the same time, Creation has just one stage and an ongoing, highly scheduled show. This show is scheduled such that very few things run concurrently, especially for the Big Name Guests. On Sunday—the day that "The Boys" Jared Padalecki and Jensen Ackles speak at the con (for Larsen and Zubernis "the mood at the convention is always different" on Sunday[26])—the schedule almost completely revolves around them:

- The special "Gold members only" panel with the boys starting the two from 10:00–10:30 a.m;
- Photo ops from 10:45–11:30 a.m. (Ackles), 1:00–1:45 p.m. (Padalecki), 11:45 a.m.–12:45 p.m. (both), and 2:00–3:00 p.m. (both with Misha Collins);
- Private meet and greets (sold at auction) from 11:00–11:30 a.m. (Padalecki) and 1:15–1:45 p.m. (Ackles);
- Panel with Padalecki and Ackles from 3:15–4:15 p.m;
- More photo ops of "The Boys" from 4:45–5:45 p.m;

- Autographs from 5:50 p.m. (with Padalecki) and 6:45 p.m. (with Ackles) until 8:30 p.m. or later.

In fact, almost all the speakers preceding *The Boys* spoke about Jared and Jensen (like the fans, always using their first names). They were the major topic of the convention throughout the three days, and their absence always displaced the speaker currently present on stage. The convention is literally about Padalecki and Ackles and functions as a celebration of them and their association with the show (even producer Robert Singer, in a rare appearance at a convention, took a moment to talk about how wonderful they were). I do not mean to suggest that Jared and Jensen *are not* wonderful people, but rather that this indicates simply how formalized the centrality of the actors are to the convention and how reliant the convention is on the proper fan response to them. Indeed, one of the "jokes" of the panel preceding Padalecki and Ackles, offered by moderator Richard Speight, Jr., was that the people in the back of the enormous theater ("Thank you for coming and putting your hard earned dollars towards…that con over there! Everyone on that stage looks so small!") would miss the "delightful musk" of the two actors.

As if mirroring the emphasis on intellectual property of the media creators, Creation also attempts to moderate fan reactions at the convention, including the display of large text on the video screen policing fan questions (Fig. 2.2). The symbolism here could not be clearer: the words on the screen literally overlay the celebrity; the policies of policing outweigh the experience of fans' seeing celebrities. Zubernis and Larsen tie this type of fan disciplining into Malin's own time as a fan: "Malin is perhaps the ultimate BNF (Big Name Fan), setting up the convention space with certain parameters which, to some extent, reduce fan shame. Male acceptance then becomes important to the (mostly female) fans as a means of validating female fan practices."[27] However, I would argue that rather than reducing fan shame, Malin actually channels shame into more authorized ways to behave, moving from fan to something-more-than-fan. In fact, Creation Entertainment started from Malin's own celebratory behavior as a comics fan, and today seems to reward fans for following the same type of celebratory fandom. Malin argues that his "deep knowledge of the genre, of the movies and the shows, of their continuities, informs me in the decisions that I make, the properties I want to work with, and the ways in which I'm able to dialogue and converse with my audience and my show demographics." As a teenager, he was a fan of Marvel comics of the

Fig. 2.2 Text on screen at *Supernatural* convention (Photo by the author)

1960s, and when he was 13, ran his first comic convention in New York City. Creation's space in some ways is Malin's own fannish space.

If Malin created his own space for his fandom, the same can be said of fans at the *Supernatural* convention—but Malin's space is different from many fans' today. Johnslynn, a cosplayer who was dressed in an elaborate Castiel costume, complete with extendable wings, argues that fandom is about finding a space of one's own:

> Regardless of what I'm dressed up as, I gravitate more toward people who are interested in what I am, because I have a lot to talk about with them..... People are a lot more friendly when they have a common interest and that's what I like because people don't feel the need to have awkward conversations and try to get to know each other. You already know each other if you're a part of fandom. You don't even need to know someone's name to start a conversation with them. Because you're all here for this one thing—

Fig. 2.3 Posted ticket prices, *Supernatural* convention (Photo by the author)

> you always have that one thing to talk about. It's something that's been on for so long and there's so many different things to talk about.

SuperWhoLock offers fans another space of creative intervention, but unlike the in-person convention space, which not only costs money but also necessarily falls under the direction of others, it allows fans to create their own type of affirmational fan celebration. Sam can be as pouty as fans want; Dean can complain about his partner as much as fans can take.

Perhaps unsurprisingly, one thing that fans did want to speak about was the pricing of the tickets for the convention as well as the tiered system in place for ticket holders. When Spieght mentions the people sitting in the back of the theater, this is what he is referring to. There are four distinct types of tickets one could purchase for this convention, along with a smattering of others (Fig. 2.3).

Figure 2.3 does not include other costs, such as autographs and photos, that are sometimes included in the ticket price, but sometimes not. It also does not summarize a few other costs, such as the "front row" seat Gold ticket (which guarantees you a seat in the front row), which was $1200 for the year I attended and went up to $1400 for the year afterwards. For the $789 Gold ticket package, attendees would receive the following:

- A reserved seat in the first 15 rows in the theater (minus the front row, which costs an extra $411). Each row had 56 seats, for a total of 840 seats total in Gold;
- Autographs from nine guests (including Padalecki and Ackles, a big selling point). There were guests who did not come with the Gold package, however;
- First in line for autographs;
- Admission to a Saturday night concert;
- Early registration and early access to the dealer's room;
- A lanyard;
- Admission to the Sunday morning exclusive panel with Jared and Jensen;
- Other attributes that other ticket holders would receive, like admission to the Karaoke concert and the right to renew tickets for the same seat next year.

For the $519 Silver package, attendees would receive:

- Reserved seats behind Gold;
- Autographs with just four guests: Jared and Jensen, Mark Sheppard, and Tyler Johnson (fan favorite Misha Collins is not included);
- Access to autographs immediately after Gold ticket holders;
- Admission to a Saturday night concert;
- Early registration and early access to the dealer's room (but after Gold access);
- A lanyard;
- And the other attributes that other tiers received.

For the $260 Copper package, attendees would receive:

- Reserved seats behind Gold and Silver (these stretched back into the hall up to row XX—after the alphabet, it went AA, BB, CC, etc.);
- Admission to a Saturday night concerts;
- A lanyard;
- And the other attributes that other tiers received.

Finally, for the General Admission package (the package that I purchased for $170), I received a non-reserved seat in the theater (past row XX), and the other attributes the other tiers received, which were access to the Karaoke night, pre-registration, and access to the dealer's room.

Note that for all the tiers, no photo opportunities (photo ops) were included; all photo ops thus cost additional amounts: Jensen and Jared were $139 each and $259 together; Misha Collins was $85 ($349 if paid with Jared and Jensen) and so forth. So although one might purchase a Gold ticket in order to get closer seats to the stage, she may still find herself paying an additional couple hundred dollars for her photo ops. The thrills of the photo ops, for fans, are described by Larsen and Zubernis as "weird things. You wait in a very long line, holding the tickets that prove you've paid the requisite (and substantial) fee, hand over your purse to an unknown security person (at least you hope it's a security person), and are then instructed precisely when to step up and stand next to the celebrity already posed for the camera. The whole process is generally over in under a minute…It's about sharing space, not possessing a picture."[28] Pictures offer a tangible reminder of the fandom, in a proximate way that online fandom like *SuperWhoLock* can only attempt to mimic.

Typical fan studies research might argue that that the larger gift economy paradigms of fandom are getting overshadowed here by the commercialization of Creation Entertainment and its allegiance to a fan-as-consumer model of fandom. As described by Karen Hellekson, the "online fan gift culture" represents a return to "the notion of the gift… in the symbolic realm," where commodification is secondary to cultivating fan relationships.[29] Fans, in this formulation of fan culture, exist as participants within a culture of exchange and interaction, not commercial exploitation. Hellekson offers Fanlib.com—a notorious failed website aimed at monetizing fan work—as an example of a commercial space that attempted to intrude on this gift economy and failed.[30] Other scholars like

Suzanne Scott and Abigail De Kosnik illustrate complications within this type of gift economy, as the corporate entities can harness fandom's gifting practices for commercial gain.[31] And for Zubernis and Larsen, convention culture will also generate tensions and competitions:

> There are, of course, always audience members who will seek to sidestep the boundaries, setting themselves apart and outside the confines to some extent. Money can buy proximity, with fans who have the means buying top-dollar packages at conventions to get them seats at the front as well as access to certain events such as a dessert party or breakfast with the actors. Still others purchase entry to private meet and greets or backstage access. These latter attendees are often regarded by other fans with a mixture of scorn and envy, as any fans who ascends the hierarchy will be.[32]

Geraghty argues that "fan communities are often deeply hierarchical and involved a systematized structure of subcultural taste and political discourse," and this is definitely apparent in Creation's tiering system.[33] But Creation's economic system seems to be the flip side to what I have previously called the Digi-gratis economy, a "simultaneous existence of both [gift and market] economies as both separated and conjoined." One view of Digi-gratis economy "indicates an economic structure where money is not exchanged, but which retains elements of a market structure"; in contrast, Creation con relies on the exchange of money to simulate the affective experiences of the gift economy.[34]

But what of the fans themselves? Some fans, like Colleen, discussed the pricing as "ridiculous! I've never seen pricing like this before.... these prices are insanity," and went on to note that "the seating is totally ridiculous" and helped to fuel a tension within fan groups. "This morning there were tons of empty seats and they would not let people sit there. Which kind of stinks for everybody including the special guests that are speaking because you are literally standing in front of a bunch of empty seats, and then a bunch of people in the back." Lindsey agreed: "whenever there's like a bunch of open seats for people who apparently paid for them, but then they didn't show up, and I think we could have moved up but we weren't allowed to do." Jennifer R. notes one "incident" that happened to her that echoes Colleen's experience:

> During one of the auction periods, when there were not a lot of people in the theater, [her daughter] was on stage as a volunteer (holding up items).

> Misha [Collins] came out to auction his script, so I went up to the gold seating area to take pictures. It was maybe 1/8 full of gold ticket holders. A woman made a nasty comment, something like "Oh here are all the usual people in our aisles and seats taking pictures again; buy a ticket next time." So maybe the gold ticket holds are the tense ones!

But at the same time, as the quotation from Felschow illustrated earlier, Creation Entertainment appears to be giving fans something they cannot get anywhere else—(moderated) access to media guests who are important for fans' own sense of celebratory fandom.[35] Creation sells out of Gold and Silver packages almost every time, and only a few fans I spoke with were upset with any sort of pricing scheme. Larsen and Zubernis note that it "can be a small price to pay for the sheer thrill of the moment."[36] But other fans are more circumspect about the pricing, noting that they do not see anything amiss with it—it is to be expected, they argue. For instance, Karen, who has been coming to the convention for years, bought the Copper package because she already had "Jensen and Jared's autograph fifteen times, and all the other times I have been, even though sitting at front would be nice, it is not worth it when you have already got fifteen Jensen autographs or whatever. What am I going to do with another one?"

It appears as though Creation has sold fans the notion of the expensive experience and that most fans have accepted the commercialization *as a given part of fandom; this is simply how things are.* Colleen, in fact, even qualified her answer slightly. Although the prices at Creation were "ridiculous," she also went to Wizard World and got the *Doctor Who* "Matt Smith VIP [experience] and it was 400 dollars, which I thought was really steep. But then you also got the whole rest of the con, which was awesome. … But that was like, a very specific person—one of the few I would be willing to spend that much money." One of the consequences of the mainstreaming of fandom is that the fan experience becomes a commodity; another consequence is that fannish history—the history of the gift economy, the history of the less commercial conventions—is forgotten.

Malin made the argument that conference tiering simply gives fans what they want:

> We have very specific ticket brackets so that fans can take advantage of things like autographs and reserved seating, and locations relative to the stage and I think those things are important. But we have a subset of customers that are perfectly content to get general admission seats and that's great too.

But tiering also creates artificial hierarchies within fandom (see Chap. 4), and naturalizes an economic view of fan affect. In contrast to shows like Wizard World or Comic-Con where one might have to stand in line for hours (or days) in order to try to get a seat in a panel (and sometimes to be shut out of the panel at the last minute), Creation does

> want every attendee to have a guaranteed seat at our show, which is really paramount to us. There's a very nasty trend amongst the big shows that they sell way more tickets than they have capacity in their theatres, so it becomes this cattle call for people to wait…We strictly capacity control our shows to the number of ticket holders as to the number of seats that we have at the show; everybody gets a seat…. We prefer a smaller, more boutique style show.

Both Jennifer and Karen echo Malin's point. Karen said that "Once you pay for a ticket here you're into everything. You can just relax and go to whatever you want to" instead of stressing about whether you will get into a particular panel or not. Jennifer also noted that "When we went to Comic-Con you got one badge, and you have to get in line at a certain time—it's first come, first serve and race to the front seats. Here it was nice. I was excited about the fact we did not have to wait in line, we had assigned seats, we could come and go and know that our seats were still going to be there."

Malin notes that "Nobody has to wait in a line for hours and hours to get into a piece of programming," and that is true to an extent. However, one still waits in line a significant amount of time at the convention for photo ops, for autographs, for dealers, to get into the programming, to get to a seat, to get out of programming—the list goes on. To ask a question to one of the celebrities during their panels, attendees often wait two or more hours in line. Larsen and Zubernis describe these "endlessly long lines" as "an integral part of conventions." Conventions, they add, "are tests of stamina as much as anything."[37]

Larsen and Zubernis's description of the convention space as a site demanding of stamina is accurate, especially as it relates to what I am describing as a "fanqueue culture" at cons. For A.O. Scott, describing his experience at SDCC, the queue for panels was the formative experience:

> In other eras and societies—the Great Depression, the Soviet Union—long lines signify scarcity or oppression. In the Bizarro World that is 21st-century

> America, it's the opposite: Long lines are signs of abundance and hedonism. Much can be learned about a civilization from studying its queuing habits, and Comic-Con surpasses even the Disney theme parks in the sophistication of its crowd management and the variety of its arrangements.[38]

I am defining fanqueue culture as one of sanctioned consumerism as cultural capital. Fanqueue culture is part of every convention: consumerism is inescapable, as guests cost money, venues cost money, and convention accouterments cost money. Malin phrases his discussion of Creation's work in economic terms:

> The bottom line is we try to get venues that we think sort of match the size of our audience profile and then once we have a venue, we know what its capacity is. We carefully capacity control them in terms of the ticket sell-through that we do. I think there are a lot of perks and advantages to different ticket packages that we offer. It extends to the ways in which we structure our on-stage presentations. Our move to having house bands, having hosts that interact with the house bands makes the stage show flow more as performance art: theatrical rather than in a very stale, talking heads rote kind of presentation which… we did … when we were kids, and now at this point in our careers we want to give our audiences a theatrical experience.

When asked about the tiering and expensive tickets, Malin argued that "the fees that we pay to our talent and for our venues, for the production values we bring to our shows, are pretty much what that is all about. We have never been out to gouge people, but we do have enormous operating costs. And the talent costs in particular have grown really huge." For what Creation Entertainment aims brings to the fans, the costs influence the pricing.

What Malin notes here is an oft-forgotten consequence of the mainstreaming of fan audiences. If fandom is becoming a more acceptable and appropriate identity—something to emulate—then it also becomes something to market and commodify. It is not just conventions that profit off of fans—it is the entire media industry that reaps benefits from attached and affective fandom. Just as Malin points out, "Acceptance of the fantastic has reversed in our society and that's a great thing to see because …. now society in general gets it." Fandom has become huge—hugely popular and hugely profitable.

But this is how niche commodities and fan-brands like *SuperWhoLock* come into existence. For as the commodification of fandom reaches full force, subsets of fandom will branch out and create new texts that represent who *they* are. Perhaps the fact that *SuperWhoLock* fandom was minimal at the *Supernatural* convention was because it conflicts with the authorized fandom engendered by Creation. These new texts may be different from the traditional ones, but will often also rely on the same corporate and productive structures of the original.[39] Malin points out that these "huge subsets inside of fandom" create "different approaches to fandom," and *SuperWhoLock* recalls these approaches as an aspect of its trans-fannish fan-brand.

Conclusion

Even though Creation Entertainment creates a single stage show that fans watch for the duration of the convention, there are still pockets of fannish creativity that emerge in the convention space. Convention spaces are not singular—that is, fans can and do create their own spaces within the convention space to engage with the text as they see fit. Although Creation creates *one* show (and that show is *the* focus for the con), the fans at the *Supernatural* convention were assembling elsewhere—in the bar, in the lobby, in each other's rooms—to participate in fandom outside of the sanctioned Creation space. As Zubernis and Larsen describe of fan spaces at conventions, they are often perceived as "more intimate" than spaces at home, and "the perception at a fan convention is that fans are no longer in a mediated world—that fans are moving from the mediated space of a mass audience into a simple audience, face to face and all in the same place at the same time." This impression is illusory, they argue, as boundaries still exist—boundaries between fans and fans, between fans and celebrities, and between fans and convention owners. Yet the spaces that fans themselves create at the convention "occupy a middle ground."[40] These spaces offer fans a respite from the overly disciplinary and allow them to squee as much as they would like to, in as undisciplined a way as they want.

SuperWhoLock represents another space where fans can go to participate in fandom in their own way. *SuperWhoLock* is like the spaces at the Creation convention outside the stage show, away from the main event. Fans create those spaces as well in order to develop their own interactions and interpretations, helping to negotiate or negate the affirmational tension of an industry-run convention. Other fans may not be able to join in those physical spaces—limitations on room size, or on friendships, may dampen the "universal" feeling of fan-created spaces. Similarly,

SuperWhoLock presents a space of limited engagement for some fans—fans who do not have access to a computer, fans who are not participants, fans who *just do not get it*.

The changing paradigm of fandom in the twenty-first century—the mainstreaming of fandom—can be interpreted in many ways. In this book, and in much of my work, I have attempted to illustrate some of the uneasy ways that media corporations deal with the popularity of an audience they once tried to alienate and discipline. Creation Entertainment, similarly, has to adjust to the influx of new fans—rising ticket prices and rising costs portend a change in the type of show that will be expected by fans. Creation Entertainment has turned a fledging, two-person startup in the 1970s into a successful enterprise. For the most part, fandom becomes explicitly condoned when a show acknowledges its own fan base on television, and this process is replicated in person at Creation cons, as fans are explicitly valued for their monetary excess. In this way, Creation Entertainment's commodification of fandom turns away from *Supernatural*'s "The Family Business" to be more "The Fandom Business."

Notes

1. Hills, "Doctor Who's Travels."
2. Booth, *Playing Fans.*
3. Zubernis and Larsen, *Fandom at the Crossroads*, 25.
4. Jenkins, *Textual Poachers*; Hills, *Fan Cultures*; Booy, *Love and Monsters*; Hills, "Dalek Half Balls"; Booth, *Playing Fans.*
5. Booth, *Playing Fans*, 27–8.
6. Felschow, "'Hey, Check It Out,'" 5.4.
7. obsession_inc, "Affirmational Fandom vs. Transformational Fandom."
8. Hills, "Dalek Half Balls."
9. Larsen and Zubernis, *Fangasm*, 7.
10. See De Souza e Silva and Sutko, "Placing Location-Aware Media," for a discussion of virtuality as both simulation and potentiality.
11. http://nupao.tumblr.com/post/28246846975/this-was-a-commission-for-kazza-spexy-who-wanted-a.
12. McClellan, "Redefining Genderswap," 1.1.
13. Mikedimayuga.
14. Hills, "Dalek Half Balls," 1.1.
15. Booth, *Playing Fans*, 42.
16. Booth, *Playing Fans*; Busse, "Geek Hierarchies"; Kohnen, "'The Power of Geek.'"

17. Schmidt, "Monstrous Melodrama"; Wilkinson, "A Box of Mirrors"; Tosenberger, "'Epic Love Story'"; Åström, "'Let's us Get Those Winchesters Pregnant'"; Brennan, "Fandom is Full."
18. Geraghty, *Cult Collectors*, 93; see also Coppa, "Brief History."
19. Zubernis and Larsen, *Fandom at the Crossroads*, 82–3.
20. TWC Editor, "Interview," 1.3, 4.2.
21. Coppa, "Fuck Yeah."
22. Geraghty, *Cult Collectors*.
23. Coppa, "Fuck Yeah."
24. Geraghty, *Cult Collectors*, 93.
25. Zubernis and Larsen, *Fandom at the Crossroads*, 22.
26. Larsen and Zubernis, *Fangasm*, 99.
27. Zubernis and Larsen, *Fandom at the Crossroads*, 22.
28. Larsen and Zubernis, *Fangasm*, 104.
29. Hellekson, "Fannish Field," 114.
30. Hellekson, "Fannish Field," 117.
31. Scott, "Repackaging Fan Culture"; De Kosnik, "Should Fan Fiction Be Free?"
32. Zubernis and Larsen, *Fandom at the Crossroads*, 25.
33. Geraghty, *Cult Collectors*, 130.
34. Booth, *Digital Fandom*, 24.
35. Felschow, "Hey, Check It Out."
36. Larsen and Zubernis, *Fangasm*, 97.
37. Larsen and Zubernis, *Fangasm*, 96, 108, 131.
38. Scott, "At Comic-Con."
39. Booth, *Playing Fans*.
40. Zubernis and Larsen, *Fandom at the Crossroads*, 21, 19.

CHAPTER 3

Doctor Who Fandom: Bigger on the Inside

Abstract This chapter describes fans' affective play at Gallifrey One, a contemporary *Doctor Who* fan convention. In contrast to the *Supernatural* fan convention, where fan-created events happen outside the boundaries of Creation's stage, at the *Doctor Who* fan convention, fan-events dominate. This chapter explores two aspects of fandom at the convention: LobbyCon, the unofficial mingling of guest and fan, and ribbon culture, the exchange of ribbons for badges. Much like *SuperWhoLock* asks fans to position the fan-reading more centrally than it does any particular textual reading, LobbyCon reveals the tension between hierarchies in fandom while the garnering of ribbons highlights a transformative aspect to fan conventions.

Keywords *Doctor Who* • Ribbon Culture • LobbyCon • Convention • Fan-run

In this chapter, I further the intra-transmedia characteristics of *SuperWhoLock* by examining the *Doctor Who* convention Gallifrey One (Gally). In contrast to the Creation *Supernatural* convention, Gally is entirely fan-run, and has been for the past 27 years. In the realm of fan conventions, it is hard to imagine more diametrically opposed views than those of Creation's conventions and the fan-run convention. Creation's

P. Booth, *Crossing Fandoms*, DOI 10.1057/978-1-137-57455-8_3

conventions tend to have fewer discussion panels and concentrate all the attendee's time on the "main stage" events, such as talks and Q&A sessions by the celebrities in attendance. Many of the people I spoke with mentioned this—Sabba noted that corporate conventions are "huge and a lot of it doesn't make any sense," while Laurel mentioned that:

> There's a lot of loss to [them]. You have to stand in line all day.... You have to pick and choose what you really want to see...you have to be willing to be able to stand in line and say I might not be able to see something, which is hard when you've paid so much money to get in and stood in line the whole day and still not be able to see what you want.

Laurel's discussion of what I have called fanqueue culture in the previous chapter helps explain one of the major differences between cons: what you stand in line for. For Laurel, and for other fans attending Comic-Con, lines help to define the convention—one stands in line in order to get into a panel, or into a vendor's room, or even into the convention itself. At Gally, the lines one stood in were more often for guests' autographs and photos. Yet, Gally, in contrast to the *Supernatural* convention (and the Sherlocked event discussed in Chap. 4) includes at least three simultaneous fan discussion panels at any time during the three-day convention, as well as more intimate discussions with the celebrity guests (intimate meaning in a room seating over 2000!) as well as the main stage event.

Within *SuperWhoLock* texts, the Doctor is the ultimate authority figure, often called upon to save Sam and Dean or John Watson. However, he can also be anti-authoritarian, whimsical, and carefree. He is passionate (when in the guise of the Tenth Doctor [David Tennant]) or cheeky (as the Eleventh Doctor [Matt Smith]). Like the fans at the convention, he is both powerful and subordinate. If *SuperWhoLock* fandom rests on the intra-transmedia connections between the three different shows, then the *Doctor Who* fan base represents a meaningful interpretation of what happens when the "powerless elite" become empowered themselves.[1]

I begin this discussion by examining the role of the Doctor in *SuperWhoLock* fan art and GIFs. Then, I tie the notion of "affective play" to Gallifrey One, specifically focusing on the role of LobbyCon—an after-hours meeting of fans and guests—and fan affect.[2] Then, I examine the use of ribbons and what I am calling "ribbon culture" at Gallifrey One. A subcultural practice of distributing ribbons to attach to the underside of the attendee's name badge, ribbon culture emerges when fans trade with each other and often (good-naturedly) compete to see who can have the longest chain of ribbons. Ribbon culture is a transformative aspect of the convention, and by discussing the role of the affective play in fan communities, I uncover how the individual fan experiences that shape contemporary fan cultures can be applied to an understanding of why *SuperWhoLock* has arisen.

SuperWhoLock: Progress in Works

In *Doctor Who*, the protagonist known as "The Doctor" can change his appearance when he is close to death. The process, known in the series as "regeneration," occurs when the lead actor is replaced, and began initially as a way of continuing the series after the first actor to play the Doctor (William Hartnell) became too ill to film. As of 2015, the process has occurred 13 times, and there have been 13 canonical Doctors. Of the many Doctors, the first eight are considered "Classic," in that they appeared in the series when it first aired from 1963–1989 (with the Eighth Doctor [Paul McGann] in the TV movie in 1996). The last four—played by Christopher Eccleston, David Tennant, Matt Smith, and Peter Capaldi—make up the New Series Doctors, appearing in the continuation of the series from 2005–present. (The War Doctor [John Hurt] appeared in the 50th anniversary episode 72 and is sometimes regarded as a "missing" regeneration.) In *SuperWhoLock*, this means that the Doctor is often the most varied and vacillating character, as any visages of these actors could appear to fulfill the role of "The Doctor" in *SuperWhoLock*. Yet, of almost all of the *SuperWhoLock* texts that I have found, very few feature the Classic Series Doctors at all. It is the New Series of *Doctor Who*—more specifically, the Doctor as played by Tennant (as number Ten) and Smith (as number Eleven)—that appear most frequently. At the same time, the Doctor travels with a number of companions, and often these characters appear in *SuperWhoLock*, even if some companions travel in *SuperWhoLock* with different Doctors.

So what is the role of the Doctor in *SuperWhoLock*? In blackbirdrose's fan art example, the Doctor is piloting his TARDIS—a time machine that is larger on the inside—with the rest of the characters from the series (Fig. 3.1). Dean, sweating, says "Someone explain to me: how is this any different to flying in a goddamn airplane!?," referencing a specific moment from *Supernatural* when Dean admits to being afraid of flying. Watson,

Fig. 3.1 *SuperWhoLock* in the TARDIS, by blackbirdrose (http://blackbirdrose.deviantart.com/art/Superwholock-in-the-TARDIS-282129424)

ever helpful, asks the Doctor if he needs help, while Sherlock and Castiel look puzzled as they investigate the interior of the Gallifreyan ship.

The two characters in the background, interestingly, are not from *Sherlock*, *Supernatural*, or *Doctor Who*. Given their proximity in the image, one might naturally assume they are the Doctor's companions; but as pointed out in the comments for the image, they are representations of the two people for whom blackbirdrose created the artwork.

Here the Doctor, in his Eleventh and Twelfth incarnation, is carefree, happy-go-lucky, and whimsical—all characteristics that might be said of the portrayal of the Doctor by Matt Smith. Yet, in *SuperWhoLock* fan work that utilizes David Tennant's work as the Tenth Doctor, there is often a more subdued, emotional, and angst-ridden note, as, for example, with Fig. 3.2. In this Gif Fic, the Doctor is contacted by Sherlock to help Sam Winchester rescue Dean from the Weeping Angels. The Doctor's face and tenor in the last two panels are serious and emotional: "Sam, where is Dean? We will find him. I promise."

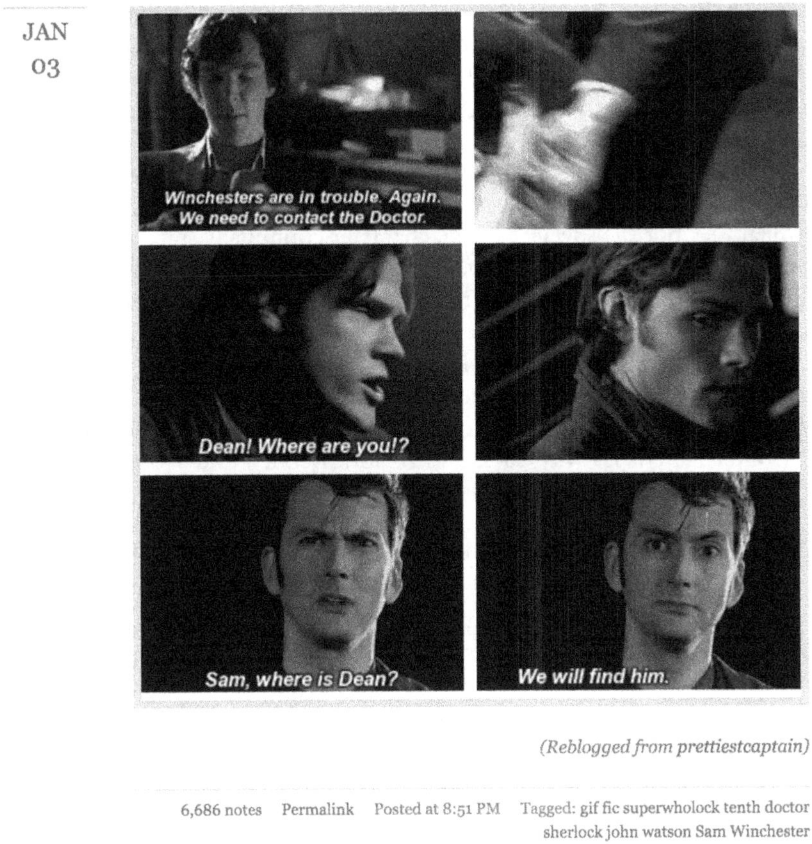

Fig. 3.2 *SuperWhoLock* Gif Fic, by prettiestcaptain (http://superwholock-gifs.tumblr.com/page/3 (original: http://prettiestcaptain.tumblr.com/post/15248052695))

The role of the Doctor in both of these *SuperWhoLock* works is similar, but the manifestation is quite different, emphasizing the importance of character. In both of these, the Doctor is a savior, come to help the Winchesters/Sherlock with a case or to transport them somewhere new. The Doctor, an alien who has powers far beyond that of a mortal human, can be the ultimate hero of *SuperWhoLock*, in the same way Castiel, as an Angel, has powers that mere mortals do not. Yet, the manner in which the

Doctor does this is portrayed quite differently in each of these texts: in one he is giddy, delirious with joy; in the other, he is serious, overtly dour. Any particular reading of any particular *SuperWhoLock* text is dependent on the reading of the Doctor, in terms of both his characterization and his incarnation.

And this is the Doctor in *SuperWhoLock*: unable to be defined or pinned down. On television, the portrayal may have some aesthetic and generic similarities, but the specifics of the character continually shift both because of the actor and because of the production team.[3] In a chapter with Jef Burnham, I discussed the way that the different actors to inhabit the role imbue it with their own personal stamp; each role is uniquely tied to the performer.[4] Unlike a character like, say, James Bond, wherein a change in the actor might signal a different *take* on the character but ultimately a very similar portrayal, the Doctor has a different personality and a different set of characteristics with each incarnation. Bennett and Woollacott demonstrate the "high degree of unity" among "Bond's persona throughout the different stages of his career," to which *Doctor Who* "affords an instructive contrast." The persona of the Doctor "has been successfully revised" through his tenure,[5] whereas Bond is "always a contemporary rather than a period figure," no matter which actor portrays the central character, as all are only interpreting "the original literary character" rather than creating something new.[6] In other words, while Bond and the Doctor are each the same character throughout their respective franchises, and each actor that has played the part has put his individual stamp on that character, each Bond is diegetically "the same" Bond while each Doctor is diegetically and markedly a different personality.[7] The Doctor is intertextuall, while Bond is intra-textual (in fact, the Doctor is more like Sherlock Holmes, who is unique in each of his multiple portrayals, although Holmes emerges in different franchises and different narratives wherein the Doctor is, ostensibly, part of the same story). At the same time, the differences in portrayal of the Doctor can lead to more or less involvement in *SuperWhoLock* texts: Amy, a *SuperWhoLock* fan and creator, describes, for instance, how the Twelfth Doctor is rarely used for *SuperWhoLock* texts because, whereas the Tenth and Eleventh Doctors "had very youthful, hyperactive personalities," the Twelfth Doctor "just hasn't found his place in that community yet."

In this way, the Doctor in *SuperWhoLock* ultimately symbolizes the intra-transmediated functionality of the *SuperWhoLock* narrative. If *SuperWhoLock* can function as an always-shifting set of narrative signifiers, each character represents both the show it was originally part of and the new text. The Doctor's own shifting portrayal enables and engages this multiplicity. Partly, these shifts may stem from the transmedia nature of *Doctor Who* itself.[8] Although not a traditional transmedia text as Jenkins might define, as "the art of world making" where one universe is constructed via "bits of the story across media channels,"[9] *Doctor Who*, as Perryman argues, "transformed itself into a flagship franchise for mainstream transmedia practices that eschew passivity for participation and static simplicity for multi-platform complexity."[10] Through *Doctor Who* fandom that kept the narrative alive during the hiatus of 1989–2005, as well as the many ancillary products—the Big Finish audios; Target, Virgin, and BBC novels; and online content—a sort of ad hoc transmedia text formed, a pattern the BBC replicated and expanded upon from 2005, when the show came back on the air.

According to Perryman, fans were crucial to this new transmedia focus as *Doctor Who*'s producers have attempted to provide "extra-value content and narrative complexity for both a hardcore fanbase and a mainstream audience by deploying a series of evolving and challenging storytelling strategies across a wide range of media platform."[11] At the same time, fans were instrumental in bringing the show back on the air, especially as many of the fans of the Classic series were active during this hiatus period and then worked on the show.[12] Indeed, *Doctor Who* fans have been an active part of the BBC's industrial strategy for years, and have played major roles in the influence of both the series and the authorized paratextual products surrounding it, buying merchandise and attending conventions, among other things.[13] It is to this active fan base that I next turn, to offer a comparative and contextual examination of the *Doctor Who* convention crowd as it relates both to *SuperWhoLock* specifically and to *Sherlock* and *Supernatural* fan audiences more generally. As with the last chapter, I begin with what Hills has called a "trans-fandom" analysis, where the multiple modes of spectatorship and affective fandom that emerge from fan audiences are put into relief with each other and create a more well-rounded and explicative enunciation of the twenty-first-century media fan.[14]

Affective Play in Fan Conventions

In this section, I briefly discuss the history of *Doctor Who* fan conventions, focus on the interaction between the fans at the convention, and argue that Gallifrey One, as the world's largest and longest-running *Doctor Who* convention, engenders a type of "affective play" between fans. But unlike the type of affective play described by Matt Hills, in which affect itself (the characteristic of an object to create emotions) becomes "playful, as capable of 'creating culture' as well as being caught up in it," the type of affective play at Gallifrey One is more indicative of a transformative play *with* affect.[15] That is, fans are not just playfully interacting with *Doctor Who*, but are playing with fandom and fan affect itself throughout the convention. The fans at Gallifrey One are enacting a particular type of *mutable habitus* that portends the type of fannish mobility undergirding *SuperWhoLock*.[16]

Like many television programs with a strong fan base, *Doctor Who* has thrived not just on the television screen, but also through celebratory fan conventions. These celebrations have taken many guises: from professionally run, BBC-organized affairs, to academic conferences, to fan/scholar celebrations of *Doctor Who*, to fan-run conventions, to record-breaking cinema extravaganzas, to fan-oriented screening parties. The sheer number of fan celebrations demonstrates the continued affective and communal power of a cult television franchise like *Doctor Who*. Lynnette Porter identifies three major fan-run *Doctor Who* conventions in the USA in 2012: Gallifrey One, the subject of this chapter; Chicago TARDIS, the one I know the best (due to proximity) and one I have written about previously; and Hurricane Who, a relatively new *Who* convention in Florida.[17] As Porter describes, *Doctor Who* conventions, even 50 years after the premiere of the show, are "thriving."[18] Indeed, in the time since Porter has written, there have been other *Who* conventions, including Re-Generation, a Mid-Atlantic convention; WhoFestDFW, a Texas convention; Long Island Who; and TimeGate in Atlanta, Ga; among many others.

In her book *The Doctor Who Franchise*, Porter describes how "some guests prefer" attending smaller events like TARDIS or other fan-run US conventions like Gallifrey One and Hurricane Who, "because they provide that personal touch and are smaller, less stressful events."[19] Rather than cloister guests in the green room or shuttle them back-and-forth in corridors underneath the hotel (or behind the hotel ballrooms), guests often walk through the crowded Dealer's room or through the hallways relatively unmolested by fans—in fact, at the 2015 Gally which I attended and researched for this book, I not only happened to walk past Nichele Nichols (Uhura from *Star Trek*) walking to her table, and had a lovely conversation with her, but also was bumped into by none other than John Barrowman, Captain Jack Harkness himself (he said "sorry buddy" and moved on as I stood, shell-shocked). At 2015's Chicago TARDIS, a friend and I had a lovely quarter hour conversation with *Doctor Who* actor Richard Franklin, who was just walking down the hallway. This sort of interaction with the guests seems natural, unforced, and engaging; the vibe of the con seems to stimulate a more laid-back approach. Of course, this vibe is cultural and socially constructed within a habitus of fandom that has been generated over 25 years of fan-run conventions.[20] In some sense, the fan actually polices herself through interpretive practices of convention-specific moments. Fans know the history of Gally—many of the fans I spoke with had been attending for many years, despite their relatively young age—and, importantly, knew the *history of the culture* of Gally. They might say to themselves that there is a history of "respect" for the guests, that they will not bother them in hallways or restroom. The implication, of course, is that *other fan groups will.* Rob noted, of a film convention in his home town, that "it was always 'the celebrity's got to stay away; we've got to put them out through the back door'" instead of Gally where you can run into guests buying merchandise. The implicit assumption—or explicit in the case of Rob—is that *other* fans will be pushy and needy, but *Doctor Who* fans are always a bit more restrained, a bit more elegant. I address this type of fan antagonism in the conclusion of the book.

Partly, the ease of access with the guests and panelists at Gally may be because of the longevity of the text itself. Apart from Barrowman and a few others from the New series of *Doctor Who* or *Torchwood*, most of the guests were from the Classic series of *Doctor Who.* They have been coming to Gally for many years and are more comfortable there. Gally has a reputation for being a safe space for celebrities. And yet, although the guests were walking through the crowd and shopping (Rob also told me that he once witnessed Eighth Docto Paul McGann shopping for playing cards with his own face on them, and chatted to him for 10 minutes), they certainly were not attending any of the fan-run panels, nor were they hanging out at Karaoke. Some of the guests did attend what is known as LobbyCon (as I discuss in more detail below), while others followed the more corporate model of attending for their sessions and then leaving the convention space.

As a model for understanding the *Doctor Who* fan audience, Gally may be a bit of an outlier. In previous years, a number of professionally run and corporate *Doctor Who* "exhibitions" have been held. As Matt Hills has described, these exhibitions are not just ways of marking a milestone for the television series, but also "epic collision[s] between fandom and brand management."[21] In general, professionally run conventions like the BBC's own 50th anniversary celebration tend to reinforce the dominant readings of the show with panels articulating authorized behind-the-scenes information or discussion with actors and crew. In contrast, smaller, more fan-run conventions tend to allow a plurality of voices, with panels discussing fannish activities like "Fandom Culture Clash" and "You Know You're a *Doctor Who* Fan When…"[22] Other *Doctor Who* fan-run conventions like Chicago TARDIS also seem to take pains to erase the barrier between fan and performer as much as possible while still maintaining a distinction between fan and celebrity.

Fan-run conventions like Gally and Chicago TARDIS assert the primacy and power of fans themselves, elevating fans from "mere consumers" to more dramatically relevant participants in the media franchise. Unlike the *Supernatural* con, which tends to shepherd fans *en masse* as consumers and passive voyeurs, *Gally* highlights the fannish aspects as just as important—or often more important—than the celebrity sessions. Stephanie, one of the attendees I spoke with, mentioned that "it's a lot more focused and fan basey …. Don't get me wrong, both types of cons are still wonderful! They just produce different atmospheres."

While certainly more fans will attend the keynote address of a major guest, it is not uncommon for some fan-panels to be attended with 50 or more in the audience. In this way, Gallifrey One demonstrates a mixture of fan and producer identities within the construction of the events. It is no surprise to learn that many of the "Doctor Who Mafia"—a group of "big name fans" from the 1980s and 1990s—have previously attended Gallifrey, as both guests and as fans (including current *Doctor Who* and *Sherlock* showrunner Steven Moffat).[23] *Doctor Who* fan discussions at conventions ascribe real change to the work of fans.

Many *Doctor Who* fans have their own "home" convention—Valoise enjoys Gallifrey One, for example, but tries to go to the much more intimate VividCon in Chicago at least every other year. Although fans of *Doctor Who* have met informally since the beginning of the show, organized fan conventions for *Doctor Who* started in earnest in the UK on Saturday 6 August 1977, with the *Doctor Who Appreciation Society*'s convention, later named Panopticon. The first US convention was held in December 1979, with Fourth Doctor Tom Baker and producer Graham Williams in attendance (there because of the last minute cancellation of the production of *Shada*). Meeting in person to celebrate the show is nothing new. The annual consistency of conventions allows them to take on new dimensions themselves, an important element now that aspects of the convention have become superfluous. Unprecedented levels of access to behind-the-scenes news, celebrity personal lives, and production details make professional conventions often a reiteration rather than a revelation of information.

Doctor Who has also seen professional exhibitions held, and as Philip Sandifer describes, these fan exhibitions are different than fan conventions.[24] In her chapter on the *Doctor Who* Experience in Cardiff Bay, Melissa Beattie points out that *Doctor Who* exhibitions have served not only to revitalize Cardiff, but also to reinforce the dominant, commercial meanings of *Who*. Indeed, unlike fan-run conventions like Gallifrey One, more official, BBC-sanctioned events tend to seem "much more like a traditional museum with... displays and structures."[25] The famous *Doctor Who Exhibition* in Longleat and the *Doctor Who Exhibition* in Blackpool were both long-running museums of *Doctor Who* props, monsters, and memorabilia.

Of all the major *SuperWhoLock* texts, it is *Doctor Who* that seems to have generated the most fan-run events, and the growing popularity of fan-run celebrations seems to be developing just as social media and the web provide copious avenues for fans to meet and congregate online. In my own research on *Doctor Who* fan conventions, I found that, for many fans, coming to Chicago TARDIS was less about meeting guests and more like "a family reunion," where they could see the friends that "got" each other's quirks.[26] That TARDIS is always the weekend of Thanksgiving increases its familial quality: Thanksgiving is to celebrate with our family, to relax by the hearth, and to enjoy the company of those—and the shows—we love. Peter Kelly and I similarly found that fan-run *Doctor Who* conventions were offline spaces where "the fans we spoke with established their 'true' fannish identity and took pride in their fandom," as opposed to online fan spaces where they still felt a modicum of shame around being a fan.[27] And Katie Booth and I demonstrated that fans at Chicago TARDIS use a discourse of authenticity—references to the perceived authentic experience of fandom itself—as a way of "demarking" the fan experience.[28]

According to its founder, Robbie Bourget, Gallifrey One started as a way to demonstrate a level of *Doctor Who* fandom in the Los Angeles area among the many other science-fiction conventions that were running at the time, including LosCon and Worldcon. In 1989, Bourget persuaded a number of local *Doctor Who* fan clubs, including the Time Meddlers, to help shoulder the financial burden of running the convention. The first guest was Jon Pertwee, who played the Third Doctor and the second was Sylvester McCoy who had only recently appeared on television as the Seventh Doctor (the show was canceled in 1989, the same year the convention started, a coincidence Bourget sarcastically calls "cleverly timed on our part"). The first Gallifrey One, co-chaired with Christian McGuire, lost money, but Bourget and McGuire borrowed from the Southern Californian Institute for Fan Interests to pay off the debt. Even from the start, the fandom circles aided each other in a financial/affective symbiosis.

From the get-go, Gallifrey One was deliberately targeted against corporate-run conventions like the *Supernatural* events that Creation runs, something Bourget calls "sanitized" conventions:

> They're very elitist. If you pay enough money you get more.... I've been to media conventions where they don't care how big the hall is, if you're not close enough to the stage—it's too bad: "I already have your money, I don't care." They don't give you a badge, nothing. Just a stamp on your hand.

Fatenah Issa, a longtime *Doctor Who* fan and conference volunteer, agrees. Having been to a Creation-run *Star Trek* convention, she notes that she prefers the fan-run:

> It was the difference between being a business run convention, and I just didn't feel a closeness or a connection, and I didn't feel a family environment as I did with the *Doctor Who* conventions. And I think that was the biggest [downside] for me. And for the Creation convention, it was basically a dealer's room, and another room with a large screen, and that was it. So the lack of variety really turned me off.

Bourget noted that the impetus for Gallifrey One was to:

> have a Doctor Who convention that was not a "media" convention—not run for profit. Not run in such a way that fans couldn't have a good time even if they weren't in the main room with the guest. So we had an art show, which most media conventions don't. And we had a masquerade, and a cabaret, and all sorts of stuff that you might find at other types of science fictions but not necessarily at media conventions. And we set that up. So you still find a gaming room, we have an art show. We have masquerade on sat night with the fans. And they get a rosette for the winner. Stuff. Because [a] convention is about fans as much as it's about the people who form and produce the show.

By any measure, Gallifrey One is one of the most successful *Doctor Who* conventions in the world. It is the largest, having grown from a crowd of 680 in 1989 to 3800 in 2015 (the maximum they will allow in order to keep it "intimate"). It is the most famous *Doctor Who* convention in the world, attracting fans from across the globe. And it has influenced and shaped other *Doctor Who* conventions, including things like cosplay contents and ribbon collection at Chicago TARDIS and other fan-run conventions.

Among the many events at Gallifrey, including the Cosplay Masquerade and the social events like karaoke or the dance party, it is LobbyCon that has become one of the most central to what I am defining as the "affective play" of the fan-run convention, and the most applicable to the relationship between *Doctor Who* and *SuperWhoLock*. In *Digital Fandom,* I described fandom as a "philosophy of playfulness," wherein fans as "participants in New Media enact the mediated communities they join."[29] The notion of this philosophy of playfulness undergirds much of the work that describes how fans interact with media objects of all kinds.[30] Indeed, the term *play* is how, in *Fan Cultures*, Hills describes the fan text: a "third space" between the inner self and the outer surface of the object of fannish desire, a space where fans can engage in play activities in both lived and created work.[31] As Börzsei points out, affective play "can help keep our inner and outer worlds separate but also connected, as well as prevent us from getting caught up exclusively in either our inner fantasy world or our external reality."[32] In other words, according to Angela Thomas, affective play is the pleasure "gained through the activities that allow individuals to challenge the boundaries between internal and external realities…that space where the fan fiction writers can experience, feel and live in a playful way within the texts that are the subjects of their fandom."[33] Play keeps us grounded and provides fans with multiple outlets for textual and intertextual experimentation. Additionally, I have shown how affective play is not just something fans engage with, it is also something that media corporations can poach from fandom itself, marketing back to fans the emotional resonance they feel toward the media text.[34]

Affective play, in these formulations, defines the relationship between fan identity and fan practice; or rather, the emotional bond between how fans identify with their fan text and their engagement with their fan activities. In this mode, then, things like cosplay and karaoke become styles of affective play engagement as fans use practice to actualize their own identities.[35] By "playing" with the different fan identities available at the convention, fans engage in the development of a fan culture.

Of all the things I spoke to fans at Gallifrey One about, LobbyCon was one of the most common refrains. LobbyCon is not unique to Gallifrey One as an unofficial "event," but it is one of the highlights of the *Doctor Who* convention for many guests. During LobbyCon, which can happen anywhere in the hotel (not just in the lobby), fans, producers, and guests mingle outside the sanctioned space of the convention throughout the evening and well into the late night/early morning hours. When I attended Gallifrey One in 2015, I sat near fellow fans and guests, including some of the major actors from the series. Fan and cosplay photographer Jonathan says that it is one of the highlights of the show. Unlike at other conventions where "the hotel had no idea what the con was about [and] ... we got kicked out of the lobby on the first day," being able to hang out with fans and celebrities "just like walking around here...that was a cool thing." It is hard to imagine that guests at the *Supernatural* con or the Sherlocked convention would mingle with the same freedom and ease—in contrast, they are often "sequestered before being escorted onstage," from panel to signing to photo shoot via out-of-bounds corridors.[36] Of course, the guests who attend LobbyCon are not (necessarily) the most current. Because of *Doctor Who*'s longevity on television, many of the guests who attend come from the early days of the series and would no longer be considered the most contemporary—New *Who* actor (and headliner) John Barrowman did not attend LobbyCon, for instance, but fan favorite actor Frazer Hines (who played Second Doctor companion Jamie McCrimmon) held court for hours.

The affective play of LobbyCon creates a different type of "third space" in which fans engage and perform their fandom. If fan communities in the twenty-first century are heterogeneous groups of disparate people, then the groups that attend fan conventions could be seen as more cohesive: the physical locality of the convention allows a geographic consistency to emerge. But LobbyCon increases this consistency, distilling the essence of fan play into a localized event. Fine and van den Scott call this sort of micro-group a "wispy community." In their discussion of different types of communities, Fine and van den Scott identify the wispy community as:

> expected to generate a surplus of fun, embedded in the memories of participants, creating sharable stories. The glasses of participants become

> rose-colored as they view their world from within the transitory wispy community. Although fun is the approved goal and result of the activity, separation from everyday life and routine identities bolsters the affective release necessary for enjoyment of the organized sociability at hand.[37]

In other words, typical academic scholarship might see Gallifrey One as a wispy community because it is time away from "everyday life," and might argue that LobbyCon is thus a microcosm of this wispiness. However, the fans I spoke with at Gallifrey seem not to see Gallifrey One in this light: rather than time "away" from everyday life, Gallifrey One is a distillation *of* their everyday life. LobbyCon is thus just a further distillation. As fandom becomes more acceptable in mainstream society, it is not unusual for fans to find ways to embrace and engage in their fannish identities outside of convention spaces.[38] Although Kelly and I found that some fans felt more shame online than they do at conventions, many of the people I spoke with said the opposite: through "offline social networks ... the fans we spoke with established their 'true' fannish identity and took pride in their fandom."[39]

This focus on the convention space being the distillation of the fan experience, not an exception from it, inherently changes the notion of affective play. Rather than seeing affective play as the interaction between *Doctor Who* and the individual fans (as we might at the *Supernatural* convention or even Sherlocked), fans during LobbyCon engage in a play *with fandom itself*. Affect—the property of an object to engender an emotional response, or that response itself as actualized within the fan—becomes a mode of interaction in the fan community. This type of affective play—an emotional connection with others that share particular characteristics with you—is not about playing "with the texts they enjoy," but about playing with the culture that embodies fandom.[40] Bourget addresses the different vibes at convention spaces:

> It's mostly the fans reacting to the set up they are in. You can get fans who behave one way at LosCon and they come to Gallifrey and they're different. Same fan, but their behavior is slightly different. What's different about it? Oh, well, here they can be a little more fanboy, then they can be at LosCon, which they feel is more serious. Okay? Isn't that a difference—because you see at LosCon, almost no one drinks alcohol. Here, there's a lot of alcohol being drunk. So that's a different matter... It's more an ambiance thing which is contributed to by all the aspects.

In other words, it is not just that the affective play of the fans creates a new experience, it is that they actually create a new conceptual space. Each convention space becomes a habitus of relations, a structural entity constructed not from the physical location but from the multitudes of practices, representations, meanings, and identities constructed for and at the convention itself. According to Navarro, the habitus is created through a social, rather than an individual process; that is, the habitus "is not fixed or permanent, and can be changed under unexpected situations or over a long historical period."[41] Just as Gallifrey One has a particular habitus in 2015, so too did it in 1989, and so will it up to and including 2063 for the 100th anniversary of *Doctor Who*. In each case, the habitus of *Doctor Who* fandom is also continually shifting and diverging, melding and adjusting. Such changes are often perceived quite negatively, especially in *Doctor Who* fandom, which has a major divide built into the series: fans of the Classic series (which ran from 1963–1989) and fans of the New series (which is currently running and started in 2005) are often perceived at odds with each other.[42] The habitus as a site of fandom appears schismatic.

SuperWhoLock becomes a habitus of fandom. Although discussion of habitus in fandom is not without precedent, such views are often themselves fractured. For example, Matt Hills discusses how fan scholars extol Bourdieu's work because "taste cultures—or specific fan cultures—can be read back into putative version of the habitus…a way of conceptualizing an individuals' consumption choices." Yet, "to follow Bourdieu is … to view media fandom as sociologically determined, disallowing any meaningful space for repertoires of fan tastes as expressions of personal identity"; that is, it eliminates the level of fandom felt at a personal, authentic identity.[43] Yet, it is precisely this authentic personal identity that the "habitus" of *SuperWhoLock* fandom allows. The affective blurring of the boundaries between creator, guest, fan, and professional during LobbyCon mirrors the blurring of boundaries in *SuperWhoLock*. The Doctor is undoubtedly a character in *SuperWhoLock*, as are the Winchesters, Castiel, Crowley, Sherlock, and John Watson. But their roles are fluid, their interactions different each time. They are not just stable entities, not just "hero" and "villain," "masculine" and "feminine," or "straight" and "gay." They are moldable, shapeable, mutable. *SuperWhoLock* is not just about the playful interaction between fan and text, it is a symbol of the way fan identities themselves are unstable, boundless entities. At Gallifrey One, I can be a presenter on a panel for one hour, a fan waiting in line to get Carole Ann Ford's signature the next, and an audience member for a headliner guest third. I can entertain and be entertained simultaneously because the convention is not segmented into categories. Just as *SuperWhoLock* creates a "third space" of intra-transmediated textuality, so too do the affective play of fan identity at Gallifrey One "unbound" the fan identity.[44] Fandom is "bigger on the inside," a boundless whole greater than the sum of its parts.[45]

A second area of affective play at Gallifrey One involves a play with particular fan hierarchies through the presentation of self via what I am calling ribbon culture. Gallifrey One (and through its influence other *Doctor Who* conventions like Chicago TARDIS) has embraced the ground-up fannish practice of fans trading badge ribbons with different sayings and images on them with other fans. Ribbons add on to ribbons to form ribbon chains, often so large they trail on the floor or have to be rolled up to avoid having catastrophic ribbon failure. Each ribbon has a different saying on it, and each might be related to something specific from the text (one I received reads "Coal Hill School Teachers," referencing the school at which companions Ian Chesterton, Barbara Wright, and Clara Oswald are teachers). Other ribbons might memorialize a person—the "Big Finish Forever Going Fo'ward ribbon was in honor of Paul Spragg, who had recently passed away—or even advertise an upcoming convention, as "L.I. Who 3" ribbon did (Fig. 3.3). Other ribbons might just be fun sayings and images that mashup or combine different aspects of *Doctor Who*, as "Scarves are cool" effectively does.

In contrast to the previous chapter, where I discussed the affirmational quality of the Creation Entertainment *Supernatural* convention, the presence of ribbon culture at Gallifrey One is a more transformative look at conventions. Few conventions even given badges to attendees, opting instead for the less expensive wristbands or tickets—but Gally's use of individualized nametags highlights its focus on the fan as an individual. Ribbons transform the badge, not to change it entirely, but to create an additional level of personalization: no fan's ribbon chain will be precisely the same as another, and each serves as a marker of one fan's particular journey though the convention space.

The ribbons are decidedly not-for-profit; no one sells ribbons at the convention. Instead, they become a way of generating face-to-face interaction, as one has to be with another fan in order to trade ribbons. Ribbons become a transformative aspect of a fannish economy of trade and exchange: to collect some ribbons, fans will have other fans engage in scavenger hunts (find all three people dressed as Zarbi, for example)

Fig. 3.3 Ribbon chain from Gallifrey One (Photo by the author)

or only give ribbons to people dressed in certain costumes. In this way, ribbon culture appears to fit squarely into what Hellekson has described as the fannish gift economy, where "to engage is to click, read, comment, write, make up a song and sing it; to hotlink, to create a video, to be invited to move on, to come over here or go over there—to become part of a larger metatext." As mentioned in the last chapter, the gift economy is not based on commercial trade or monetary exchange but rather depends on "a system of exchange based on symbolic gifts that represent the self while constituting the community."[46] Ribbons seem the ultimate gift as they cement a relationship that is visible to others ("oh, you have the 'Spoilers!' ribbon? So do I!") and also provide a way of marking the self as a community of others: everyone has ribbons, but no one will have the same number of ribbons or in the same order as anyone else.

Gallifrey One is not the only convention to use ribbons, but it has been embraced by the participants at Gally. According to Gallifrey One website, they are "absolutely *not necessary*...they have nothing whatsoever to do with the convention itself. But they certainly add to the ambience of the event." Despite arguing that the ribbons have nothing to do with the convention, the convention staff do recommend a number of vendors where fans can purchase ribbons for trade/giveaway, but they strictly enforce the semblance of the gift economy at the convention: "Ribbon distribution tends to be completely open, available to anyone...but never for any compensation. (The convention committee will frown heavily upon locating anyone selling badge ribbons for any reason, and that potentially includes removal from the event.)" Bourget describes how the ribbon culture at Gallifrey One got started:

> The first time I ever saw ribbons was at the East Coast Science Fiction convention where they were used to identify who was what. So it would say, Program Person, or Staff, or whatever. And somebody went, that's cool. The next year people started making their own. And it just grew. Now World Science Fiction conventions sort of put a bit of a cap on it—this is interesting but it's not great. Other conventions go really whole hog. Gallifrey is one where we go whole hog—one of our guests one year made a kilt out of all the ribbons he'd been given. He sat in here, with some of the girls, making this kilt. So he could wear it on stage on the last day. One of the ladies made a dress out of all the ribbons she got. We regularly auction off for the charity a ribbon chain—they go around collecting ribbons from everybody and they make a huge gigantic chain of them on a badge that says charity ribbon, and it gets auctioned, for a huge amount of money.

Although no one appeared to have a "my ribbon is longer than yours" competition at the convention I attended, there was a certain level of pride in the length of the ribbons created. Further, the ribbons echoed Kelly and my description of the reduced level of shame at fan conventions, although it is hard to imagine that many of these same proud fans wore their ribbons on the airplane home or to work the next week.[47]

Yet, despite its resemblance to the gift economy, there are aspects of ribbon play that are decidedly not. For example, ribbons are not free; one has to purchase them from any number of companies in order to present them at the convention. The set of 500 I ordered cost approximately $140—a not inconsiderable sum considering the cost of the convention, flights, and hotels. In this way, the ribbons are—like many aspects of fan culture that have been seen as part of a gift economy (e.g., digital content, zines, vidding)[48]—actually imbricated with other economies as another type of Digi-gratis economy.[49] In this economic system, goods and services may be exchanged for free, but an underlying commercial metaphor guides the exchange. Rarely did individuals make their own ribbons, and ribbons often served multiple purposes. The Gallifrey One website hints at this when it notes that:

> If you see someone quietly palming a ribbon to someone, turning their back, or otherwise engaging in a behavior suggesting they are being secretive, don't run up to them and ask for a ribbon; they could be low on ribbons, or they may have made a ribbon that is specifically given to only their friends or only to people in a certain costume.

Given this, and the fact that it is highly unlikely anyone will bring 4000 ribbons to the convention to freely give out, there remains an implicit, but not insignificant, competition couched within the action of ribbon distribution. Although I certainly enjoyed collecting ribbons, it became a stressful situation when someone would run up to you, interrupt a conversation, ask for a ribbon, and then run away again.

Ribbon culture affectively plays with the notion of fannish commodification by most deliberately (and yet only ostensibly) existing outside of commodification practices. In other words, fans utilize a conception of the gift economy, but end up de-gifting it; at the same time, they de-commercialize the commercial economy. Trading and collecting ribbons becomes a social force of good-natured competition: although length may not be explicitly compared, it is often judged. Put another way, collecting ribbons is both like and unlike collecting other types of merchandise; one can collect ribbons as a way of generating affect in the "solid signifiers of the historical significance of previous media texts," but the ribbons will always be a type of "Fannish fiction," a term Godwin uses to describe fan practices "not defined by ... existing mass media texts, characters, narratives or worlds."[50] Although the ribbons are *about Doctor Who,* they are not *of Doctor Who.* In this case, ribbon culture becomes a parody of commercial economics, but the act of giving ribbons becomes a pastiche of gift economies.[51] It is a commodity without the text: fans' giving of ribbons becomes a type of affective play with the mechanisms and facilitates of fandom itself.

Conclusion

SuperWhoLock represents the nature of the contemporary, digital fan audience. Like the Doctor himself, who changes and regenerates every few years, the *Doctor Who* fan audience is equally mutable, finding itself as both part of larger fan practices and engaging in unique fan practices. Ribbons were a uniquely Gallifrey One event—they did not appear at Creation Entertainment events (partly because Creation does not give participants badges) nor did they appear at Massive Event and Showmasters' Sherlocked convention.

The affective play of ribbon culture becomes linked to the culture of *SuperWhoLock* fandom; for *SuperWhoLock* is nothing if not intertextual and yet there is no overt corporate commodification of it at all. *SuperWhoLock* is a crossover commodity without commodification. Because it exists at the nexus of multiple fan contexts, and nowhere in professional contexts, *SuperWhoLock* cannot be commodified except by fans themselves in non-sanctioned spaces like Etsy. It represents a play with the commodification of fandom as fans engender their own engagement with the requisite texts. Any *SuperWhoLock* entities—physical representations of *SuperWhoLock*—become conflated with the text itself. *SuperWhoLock* is a text only inasmuch as the creations suggest; and thus complicates fannish commodification. Rather than focusing on the deployment of *SuperWhoLock* across multiple media outlets, one must necessarily understand all *SuperWhoLock* "merchandise" as existent in the same demediated culture.[52] *SuperWhoLock* is only as whole as its fans construct it to be.

But the affective play of fans at Gallifrey One was something shared, in various aspects, with other fan groups at the other conventions.

SuperWhoLock appears to sit at the intersection of three fandoms that all engage in "playing fans" in different ways.[53] At the *Supernatural* convention, the space of the convention itself became a site of affective play, as the fans moved outside the bounds of the official main stage event to create their own pockets of conversation. And, as I will demonstrate in the next chapter, fans at the Sherlocked convention responded to overt cultural hierarchies as a similar form of affective play.

Notes

1. Tulloch and Jenkins, Science Fiction Audiences, 145.
2. Hills, *Fan Cultures.*
3. Hewett, "Who is Matt Smith?"; see Chapman, *Inside the TARDIS*; Hills, *Triumph of a Time Lord*; but Booth, "Periodising *Doctor Who.*"
4. Booth and Burnham, "Who Are We?"
5. Bennett and Woollacott, *Bond and Beyond*, 275–6; Tulloch and Alvarado, *Doctor Who*, 198–205, 275–6.
6. Chapman, *Licence to Thrill*, 17–18.
7. With the caveat that some meta-jokes enter the narrative, for example, George Lazenby looking at the camera in *On Her Majesty's Secret Service* and saying "This never happened to the other guy," referencing Sean Connery.
8. Perryman, "*Doctor Who.*"
9. Jenkins, *Convergence Culture*, 21.
10. Perryman, "*Doctor Who*," 22.
11. Perryman, "*Doctor Who*," 36.
12. Hills, *Triumph of a Time Lord*, 54–84.
13. Hills, "Dalek Half Balls"; Hills, *Unfolding Event*; Booth, ed. *Fan Phenomena.*
14. Hills, "Doctor Who's Travels."
15. Hills, *Fan Cultures*, 93.
16. Bourdieu, *Logic of Practice*; see Hills, "'Patterns of Surprise.'"
17. Porter, *Doctor Who Franchise*; Booth, "First Time"; Booth, "Cultural Lives"; Booth and Kelly, "Changing Faces."
18. Porter, *Doctor Who Franchise*, 149.
19. Porter, *Doctor Who Franchise*, 151.
20. Bourdieu, *Logic of Practice*; Navarro, "Cultural Interpretation of Power."
21. Hills, "Cultural Lives."
22. See Booth, "Cultural Lives."
23. Hills, *Triumph of a Time Lord.*
24. Sandifer, "You Were Expecting Someone Else."

25. Beattie, "'Doctor Who Experience,'" 178.
26. Booth, "The First Time."
27. Booth and Kelly, "Changing Faces," 57; Zubernis and Larsen, *Fandom at the Crossroads.*
28. Booth and Booth, "Discourse of Authenticity."
29. Booth, *Digital Fandom*, 192.
30. Booth, *Game Play.*
31. Hills, *Fan Cultures*, 111.
32. Börzsei, "Playing in the Sandbox," 10.
33. Thomas, "Fan Fiction Online," 236.
34. Booth, *Playing Fans.*
35. Lamerichs, "Stranger Than Fiction."
36. Zubernis and Larson, *Fandom at the Crossroads*, 25.
37. Fine and Van den Scott, "Wispy Communities," 1323.
38. Sandvoss, *Fans*; Booth, *Playing Fans*; although not completely accepted, see Busse, "Geek Hierarchies"; Hills, "'Twilight' Fans."
39. Booth and Kelly, "Changing Faces," 57.
40. Thomas, "Fan Fiction Online," 235.
41. Navarro, "Cultural Interpretation of Power," 16.
42. Newman, *Doctor Who*; Hills, *Triumph of a Time Lord*; Booth and Kelly, "Changing Faces"; but Booth and Booth, "Discourse of Authenticity."
43. Hills, "'Patterns of Surprise,'" 817–8.
44. Hellekson, "'Doctor Who Unbound.'"
45. Thomas, "Marrying."
46. Hellekson, "Fannish Field of Value," 113, 116.
47. Booth and Kelly, "Changing Faces."
48. Noppe, "Commodifying Fan Work."
49. Booth, *Digital Fandom.*
50. Geraghty, *Cult Collectors*, 2; Godwin, "G.I. Joe V.s Barbie," 112.
51. Booth, *Playing Fans.*
52. Booth, *Digital Fandom.*
53. Booth, *Playing Fans.*

CHAPTER 4

Sherlock Fandom: The Fandom Is Afoot

Abstract This chapter on *Sherlock* fandom focuses on the fan convention Sherlocked as a manifestation of economic hierarchies in fan cultures. The Holmesian oeuvre of Sir Arthur Conan Doyle sits in an uneasy position between popular and high culture, and this chapter probes this tension through the lens of *SuperWhoLock* as an example of fan hierarchies. This chapter ties the cultural hierarchies in *SuperWhoLock* fandom to the economic and class hierarchies of the convention.

Keywords *Sherlock* • Convention • Hierarchies • Economics • Class system

The character of Sherlock Holmes is one of the most famous in all of English literature. Beyond print, his tales have spread to radio, film, television, and board games, among other media.[1] Sherlock Holmes is also one of the original emphases of fan cultures: born from the writing of Arthur Conan Doyle, Holmes developed his own fandom in the late nineteenth century, and became one of the first popular fictional characters to inspire fans.[2] The power and pervasiveness of Sherlock Holmes fandom can be seen as far back as 1893 and the publication of Doyle's "The Final Problem": Holmes falls to his death at the end of the story, and as Balaka Basu argues, "caused distraught readers to wear black armbands in unprecedented mourning for a fictional character." That Conan Doyle brought

P. Booth, *Crossing Fandoms*, DOI 10.1057/978-1-137-57455-8_4

Holmes back in *Hound of the Baskervilles* in 1903 "[demonstrated] for perhaps the first time, the power that readers can exert over a narrative in which they are invested."[3] In an interview with me, Holmesian fan-scholar Pat agreed, describing how "people mourned" when Conan Doyle "killed off Sherlock." According to Roberta Pearson, the first official Sherlockians (the society of Sherlock fans/aficionados) "gathered at a New York City drinking establishment in 1934," although fans had been meeting in the UK informally earlier than that.[4]

As part of *SuperWhoLock*, the television series *Sherlock* is resplendent in fan trappings: as Matt Hills has described, *Sherlock*'s "mention of 'fan sites' playfully gestures to Holmesian knowledge, suggesting that the exegesis of TV fans is valuable and worthy of the great detective's attention."[5] If fandom was important to Conan Doyle's success, it is crucial for *Sherlock*'s. Of all the cult fan texts that thrive today, it is Sherlock Holmes that reveals the longevity and survival of fandom across decades, through multiple media representations, and with varied (and often surprising) portrayals.

It is no surprise, then, that a convention based on the 2010 BBC production *Sherlock* would have a strong fan audience and, at the same time, that this audience would not necessarily be in agreement about what aspects of *Sherlock* were conducive to *SuperWhoLock* production. If in the last chapter I emphasized the fan-run nature of Gallifrey One, the *Doctor Who* convention, as well as the hierarchy invoked via ribbon culture, in this chapter I continue my exploration of fandom as a fluid and multifaceted identity by discussing the fan hierarchies that develop through perceived economic classism within media fandom. The Holmesian oeuvre of Sir Arthur Conan Doyle sits in an uneasy position between popular and high culture, and this chapter will probe this tension through the lens of *SuperWhoLock* as an example of fan expertise. I examine this expertise through the experiences of fans at the first major *Sherlock* fan convention, Sherlocked, held in late April 2015 in London.

Relating fan hierarchy to economic status is nothing new. In 1992, Jensen noted that the stereotyping of fandom as a pathological malady stemmed partially from a desire to distinguish "them" (fans) from "(the more reputable) patrons or aficionados or collectors," clearly demonstrating an economic basis to this stereotype.[6] Today, fan hierarchies often also hinge on the relative closeness of *the* fan to *a* perceived conception of *a* fan created by the media industries. Bourdieuian analysis, a look at social hierarchies in taste, is "rooted in a central and guiding metaphor….that cultural life can be modeled by taking an 'economisitic' approach." Hills' analysis of Bourdieu in fan studies is an authoritative take on the way that social hierarchies can replicate economic ones, but with a significant shift: cultural capital, the hierarchies established within fan cultures "may, at any single moment of culture-in-progress, remain variously fragmented, internally inconsistent and struggled over."[7] Roberta Pearson later augments this critique, arguing that value as applied to fandom can shift and change as historical perspectives do.[8]

The problem with ascribing value through economic models within fan analyses is that it automatically (reductively, and a posteriori) values commerical value over other types of value (e.g., knowledge, community, participatory).[9] This is precisely what happened at the Sherlocked fan convention in London. The extreme financial hierarchy at the convention developed via a replication of the economic stereotypes of fan communities. As I describe in this chapter, the pricing scheme at the convention, which ranged from a day pass of £29 to a "VIP" pass of £2995, effectively forced *Sherlock* fans into a financial class system, echoing Bourdieuian views of fan cultures.

In this chapter, I want to focus on how these key impulses, investments, and practices (a) are manifest through the characters of Sherlock Holmes in *SuperWhoLock* fiction, art, and Tumblr posts; (b) are negotiated at the economically hierarchical Sherlocked convention in 2015; and (c) are understood by the diverse group of fans that created the "Unlocked" Tumblr online convention, in response to Sherlocked. Throughout, I expand on recent fan studies literature about the role of hierarchy and cultural capital in fan communities by comparing *SuperWhoLock* as a multi-fan experience and fluid identity with an examination of the corporate Sherlocked.[10] I hope to reveal the multiplicity at the heart of the contemporary fan, and to develop the metaphor of *SuperWhoLock* as key fan text moving forward in fan studies.

SuperWhoLock: Progress in Works

Just as with *Doctor Who* and *Supernatural*, *Sherlock* is an odd addition to the *SuperWhoLock* canon. Sherlock Holmes has a much longer literary tradition to fall back upon than does *Supernatural*, and *Sherlock* is very much tied to the everyday (if extraordinary) realities of life, as opposed to *Doctor Who*'s more fantastical narratives. *Sherlock* does not include demons, aliens, monsters, or beings with usual powers (excepting Sherlock and his amazing powers of deduction, of course). *Sherlock*'s world is augmented by technology—"the introduction of digital logics like search and filter into Sherlock Holmes' tool set impacts what we might mean by Sherlock's 'science of deduction'"[11]—but his powers of deduction are based in real-world (if often unbelievable) manifestations of that "appropriation of technology."[12]

Yet, both because *Sherlock* has the same showrunner as does *Doctor Who*, Steven Moffat, and because it includes a character to whom the audience can connect within the *SuperWhoLock* narrative, there are clear ties between the series that manifest in *SuperWhoLock* fiction: "the open-ended nature of each show's narratives" allows for multiple readings of the characters, events, plots, and moments to be coded and recoded.[13] That Sherlock both died (because in 1893 he had) and did not die (because Doyle resurrected him in *The Hound of the Baskervilles*) at the end of the "Final Problem" means the narrative open-endedness of the *character* Sherlock is inscribed in canon for purist fans; that *Sherlock* the television series has developed a hyperdiegesis within the fictional world translates this open-endedness to modern audiences.[14] At the same time, the open-endedness of *Sherlock* is qualitatively different than that of *Supernatural* and *Doctor Who*—as Hills describes, it is "fractured and fragmented across parallel versions" rather than deepening and extending—"less a folding or unfolding text than a torn text."[15] In practice, this means that Sherlock as a transmedia character takes on multiple forms, but *Sherlock* as a series is a pastiche of these multiple versions, a fan fiction of a hyperdiegesis, facilitating a greater fluency with the Sherlock Holmes canon.[16]

The pastiche of *SuperWhoLock* is based both on semantic reproduction of textual elements from *Sherlock*, *Supernatural*, and *Doctor Who* and on a syntactic appropriation of ideological moments from each media text.[17] In terms of *Sherlock*, the extraordinary observational and deductive powers of the titular detective help frame and contextualize the way fans' own knowledge and competencies about their favored shows manifest.[18] That is, fans' expertise becomes akin to Sherlock's own intellectual gifts, and the fans that construct *SuperWhoLock* demonstrate this connection to the text(s).[19] This is not to say that the character of Sherlock in *SuperWhoLock* becomes an exact double for the fans' own experiences, but that because of the character's mutability—his ability to shift characteristics depending on the manifestation of the text (be it BBC's *Sherlock*, CBS's *Elementary*, Warner Brother's *Sherlock Holmes* movies, etc.[20])—fans have a kind of freedom to make Sherlock into whatever suits their purposes.[21] Faye argues that fans of *Sherlock* and fans of Sherlock Holmes "are called to something similar at heart, and the details [of the texts]—however beloved—have been proven disposable"; indeed, she notes that "Sherlock Holmes as a popular heroic figure displays a remarkable level of tantalizing opacity."[22] Fandom can be about appreciation as much as appropriation, and Sherlock Holmes fandom began with affective appreciation of the text itself: for example, Stein and Busse describe the way fandom has been present in Sherlock Holmes communities since the earliest days of the stories, while Anne Jamison describes the types of fan activities undertaken by these Sherlock Holmes fans.[23]

Although as Stein and Busse state, "regardless of terminology and self-understanding, diverse *Sherlock* fans share many key impulses, investments, and practices," it is also important to note that hierarchies always exist within fan communities.[24] The show *Sherlock* itself could be considered a high-culture riff on the works of Arthur Conan Doyle, as *Sherlock* creators/writers Steven Moffat and Mark Gatiss are both admitted fans of Doyle's work. Fans of the Great Detective have been writing fiction about Sherlock Holmes for decades, although as Ashley Polasek offers, such "pastiches" are often considered more "high class" than the (lower class) "fan fiction" of contemporary writers. "The differences," she writes, "between pastiche and fan fiction have generated tension within the Sherlockian community...Before the Internet, authors had limited options for disseminating their work and traditional publishing methods have acted in a sense as quality control for pastiche." Pastiche is imitative of the original Doyle; fan fiction is not beholden to this great imitation game and is therefore degraded by purists. While Moffat and Gatiss do not strive for authentic Doyle in their updated take on the detective stories, their work "is able to offer a wider scope for unencumbered and much broader fan discourse."[25] Moffat and Gatiss's familiarity with the canon of Conan Doyle appealed to some of the fans I spoke with at Sherlocked. Pat, a psychologist who likens Sherlock's style of deduction to her study of dementia patients, says that "if you look for it, you can see that not only are [Moffat and Gatiss] doing the canon, but they're also doing the experience of it. So for me this isn't flashy, this is very intelligent."

I met many fans who had written or read fan fiction based on Sherlock Holmes (and not necessarily just the current television series). Pat's fandom of Holmes (she described herself as a Holmesian, not just a fan of *Sherlock*) describes the power of Holmes fan fiction in the 1950s for her father:

> My dad was gay and he and his partner, even in the 1950s, would go to gay pubs to read Holmes and to discuss it. And that's in the 1950s. They'd come down to London, they'd go to the gay bars in London, and there'd be Sherlock Homes readings that would talk about them being closeted even then. …Because in the 1950s, he'd be in his 20s, there'd be men there at the meetings who were in their 60s and 70s. And they report talking about the gay reading of Sherlock Holmes back in the 1920s! But you couldn't write it down, you couldn't publish it. But that didn't mean it didn't go on underground.

Polasek notes that "the homoerotic subtext of the series is one of the most explored themes in *Sherlock* fan fiction," and something that *SuperWhoLock* fans latch onto, often in an attempt to subvert the original text's queer-baiting of Holmes/Watson slashers.[26]

The multifaceted character of Sherlock Holmes is ideal for *SuperWhoLock*:[27] as Francesca Coppa describes, from his very beginnings Holmes was a "transmedia figure," constructed from combinations of text and image (drawn from the pictures drawn for *The Strand*) that are "at least partly responsible for the ease and rapidity with which Holmes transcend text."[28] In the same volume, Louisa Stein and Kristina Busse call him "an evolving transmedia figure, at the center of myriad cultural intersections and diverse representational and fan traditions."[29] Their definition of transmedia moves beyond Henry Jenkins's classic definition of a media narrative dispersed across multiple outlets, and instead sees a transmedia text (or, in this case, character) as one for which "audiences as well as official authors co-construct … narratives, storyworlds, and frames for engagement."[30] Later, they redefine his role as "of the outsider who uses but isn't fully part of the system" as "an appealing attribute for a main character as identificatory figure."[31] Fans that I spoke to at the Sherlocked convention noted this connection to the character: Vidalie, a fan from France who came to London for the con, noted that fans of the series "share…Sherlock," or at least the version of Holmes in the show. Ben, a fan from the UK and knowledgeable about "the character from the works of Doyle," described being a fan of the series largely because of "the way that Benedict [Cumberbatch] and Martin [Freeman] choose to portray the characters. I like the fresh take on it."

Sherlock Holmes is often placed within the *SuperWhoLock* canon as a figure both erudite and alien. For fans, this characterization invites "fan and scholar-fan participation in (extra-) diegetic worlds of knowledge, through which the character of Sherlock and the textual values of *Sherlock* can be actively appropriated."[32] In other words, Holmes's own knowledge as filtered through his cyborgian interaction with networked technology presents a character that is not necessarily always aware in advance of what he knows, but rather can find information using digital technology and social media.[33] In many ways, Sherlock's journey through digital technology mirrors fandom's own experiences. As Pat explains, her fandom manifested first through "things like the fanzines.... And then [she] went into chat rooms and then eventually [she] went to Tumblr. And now it's Tumblr and Twitter, really." *SuperWhoLock* fandom demonstrates the same usage—and mastery—of technology as does Holmes himself.

Indeed, Holmes in *Sherlock* is a representation of both fan knowledge acquisition and an overt brusqueness that comes with the character's anti-social nature. This matches in *SuperWhoLock* with the ways that the Doctor's portrayal reveals a similar antipathy for humankind, or Dean's general grumpiness. The similarities between the Doctor and Sherlock Holmes were expressed by many of my interview subjects—and in a commentary on the audio version of *The Final Problem*, director and star Nicholas Briggs offers this summary of those characteristics:

> As many people have said, there are similarities between the character of the Doctor and Sherlock Holmes and certainly I think a lot of writers have muddied the waters between the two in terms of the way the characters behave. Because essentially, it's that role in a mystery where there is a character who has lots of special knowledge and is slightly mysterious and deals with people on a slightly eccentric, different level.[34]

One of the people I interviewed at Gallifrey One, Cinnamon Hayes, simply summed it up as: "the Doctor and Sherlock probably have the same mental disorder." This mysteriousness and eccentricity manifests in *SuperWhoLock* in many ways. For example, in Fig. 4.1, in a work of art by Tumblr artist hoursago, Dean Winchester angrily points to the Eleventh Doctor, leaning against the doors of the TARDIS, and cries "Look, I don't care what color your porta-potty is, I'm not gettin'..." Sherlock

Fig. 4.1 Sherlock hears all, by hoursago (http://hoursago.tumblr.com/post/15844762950/i-want-to-get-in-on-this-team-free-willteam)

Holmes, as personified by Benedict Cumberbatch's portrayal, responds, his back to the pair, "It's colour," emphasizing the British spelling of the word as opposed to Dean's American spelling.[35] Flabergasted, Dean derogatorily notes both the Eleventh Doctor (Matt Smith) and Sherlock (Benedict Cumberbatch) "cheekbones," drawing attention to the actor's shared facial structure (although as Dean is played by Jensen Ackles, a man who is no stranger to cheekbonage himself, the insult is mild at best).

The snarky reply from Sherlock emphasizes a number of aspects of this character as it represents the trans-fandom within *SuperWhoLock*. First, Sherlock's desire to correct other character's words and ideas transcends even written knowledge itself: here, Sherlock appears to be able to "hear" the spelling of the word, or can somehow communicate telepathically with the others—a rather alien and/or supernatural ability, this "telepathy" allows the character to fit in with the other two texts more deliberately. Like the Doctor, Sherlock demonstrates that he can read minds, or at least has a modicum of psychic powers; like the world of *Supernatural*, here Sherlock reveals an ability that is more than human.

Conversely, a different reading of this interaction could reveal instead that Sherlock is *not* mind reading, but is in fact able to actually *read the text bubble above Dean's head*. The meta- (self-referential) nature of *SuperWhoLock* becomes obvious in this reading of the short cartoon. *SuperWhoLock*, both because of its crossover nature, and also because the texts upon which it is based are often self-referential, can reflect back and comment on itself or on the shows upon which it is based. Characters reference tropes or stereotypes from each other's shows—fans define characters by their experiences in the particular shows they reference. The fact that Sherlock here can read Dean's bubble to know the spelling reveals a self-referentiality within the texts themselves. *Supernatural*, in particular, has become known for breaking the fourth wall, as characters within the show have become aware of a series of novels based on their adventures that exist within the diegesis, and which have formed fans of their own.[36]

Third, Sherlock can perhaps interpret the American spelling from Dean Winchester's accent, revealing the UK/US tension inherent in *SuperWhoLock*: that, as many fans have noted (including many people I interviewed at Sherlock), both *Doctor Who* and *Sherlock* seem to fit well in the same universe because they are British, but the American *Supernatural* does not seem to fit. Indeed, the connection between *Sherlock* and *Doctor Who* goes deeper than mere nationality and beyond the fact that Steven Moffat is the showrunner of both. For C.B. Harvey, for instance, a wealth of intertextual and transmediated connections between *Doctor Who* and the Sherlock Holmes stories reveals a "flow moving from the original Sherlock stories and their adaptations via the classic series of *Doctor Who* and its spinoff media, which in their turn inform post-2005 *Doctor Who* and, by extension, the *Sherlock* series."[37] According to media historian James Chapman, the Doctor has "more than a suggestion of Sherlock Holmes in his characterization." Such characteristics include tinkering in his laboratory, impatience with "those whose intellect does not match his own," treating authority figures with contempt, and having extreme eccentricities.[38] Harvey describes "the Sherlockian archetypes and iconography encountered by *Doctor Who*'s eponymous adventurer, even extending to story-telling strands that stretch from the Detective's world to the Doctor's universe," relating the two protagonists through narrative style.[39]

This "enduring relationship" between the two franchises has developed into its own unique textual diegesis, *WhoLock*. The term, like *SuperWhoLock*, seems to have developed in January 2012, but became most popular in December 2013 with the release of a superbly edited fan-made video called "WhoLock—Sherlock meets The Doctor!" by John Smith. Viewed as of 2015 over 4 million times, the video consists of spliced together footage from Matt Smith's portrayal of the Eleventh Doctor with Cumberbatch's Sherlock. The description of the video from YouTube reads: "Months after an encounter with a mysterious 'Doctor', Sherlock becomes obsessed with discovering more about this impossible man… until the man makes an unexpected return."[40] Upon hearing the TARDIS dematerialize, Sherlock goes outside to investigate. The Doctor closes the door, and Sherlock approaches the blue box, all while Watson looks at them from the street. The matching of footage between the two shows is extraordinary, as the character of Sherlock literally does appear to walk through the TARDIS doors while the Doctor is in shot. There is an inherent remix effect to this video, as images of the Doctor are taken from multiple episodes/costumes/hairstyles of the Eleventh Doctor (the floppy-haired Doctor from the Fifth Series contrasts with the more gelled coif of the Seventh Series [the "VFX Breakdown" video that John Smith posted afterward reveals the majority of the clips are from the episode "Hide"]), and some of the vocals and lip movements have been dubbed from different episodes.

In some ways, *WhoLock* was more well known to the British fans at Sherlocked than *SuperWhoLock*: so much so, in fact, that Steven Moffat addressed rumors that an official *Doctor Who/Sherlock* crossover was in the works (it is not).[41] Neither Ben nor Thom knew much about *SuperWhoLock*, for instance, although they knew of *WhoLock*. Ben describes the video noted above as "really well done," but does not "think *Supernatural* has a big a presence … in the UK as it does in the US. It certainly is well known within the community that's [at Sherlocked]. But certainly [in the UK], *Doctor Who* and *Sherlock* are institutions, which *Supernatural* isn't. But I can certainly see how fans see the appeal of all three." Sarah, an American studying in the UK, feels as though "*Supernatural is* America to me. And it's an American. .. for some reasons that doesn't match the English for *Sherlock*, and for *Doctor Who*." *Supernatural* is a representation of Americana, from the run-down motels frequented by the Winchesters to the "small towns" often visited on the show. Tanya, a British fan, prioritizes the shows: *Sherlock* comes first, then *Doctor Who* ("mainly because my husband watched *Doctor Who*"), but she had "not seen anything from *Supernatural*, except for things online and I just think I don't have enough time. There's not enough space in my life for three fandoms, I just have to watch the one."

Yet, although the fans did not like (or watch much) *Supernatural*, they did all *know* it. This statement mirrors what Perez describes of *SuperWhoLock* fandom: being part of one fandom and seeing *SuperWhoLock* online teaches fans about the others.[42] For British fan Nicole, *SuperWhoLock* was actually how she got into the other shows—enjoying those other shows separately/independently from the crossover of *SuperWhoLock*. Her "first URL on Tumblr [was] *SuperWhoLock*. … [But] then it just gets to the point where it's like, well, I don't want to put them together any more. I want to keep them separate."

The UK connection extends to *Sherlock* fandom in other ways. Pat only watches *Doctor Who* for the crossover effect highlighted by Steven Moffat's participation in both. She thinks "Moffat gives me clues about what's going on in *Sherlock* in *Doctor Who*. So there are several of us who watch *Doctor Who* just for the clues to *Sherlock*." She points to some specific connections—"lines of dialogue that were identical" and plot points that matched up. "That can't be the writer being lazy, because he's too clever for that," she claims, "that's him giving you hints, what's going on here, is what's also going to go on there." Her reading of the duality of the shows stems from Moffat's desire "to mirror things. Even in the show, but he's doing it now with the duality of the two shows"—mirrored characters ("cheekbones"), mirrored plots, mirrored lines of dialogue (see Fig. 4.2).

Fig. 4.2 Gif set of similar dialogue, by Marco (http://faithfulviewer.co.vu/post/92737158825/doctorsherlock-parallels-i-dont-like-not)

At the same time, *SuperWhoLock* fans note a major absence within *Sherlock* that conversely ties *Doctor Who* more strongly to *Supernatural*: the use of actor Mark Sheppard. Sheppard is well known in cult fandom for playing important roles in many sci-fi and action series over the past 20 years (*X-Files*, *Firefly*, *Supernatural*, *Battlestar Galactica*, *Leverage*, *Doctor Who*, *Star Trek: Voyager*, et al.). In *Supernatural,* he plays Crowley, the king of Hell; in *Doctor Who,* he plays a young Canton Delaware III (his father, W. Morgan Sheppard, played the older version of Canton Delaware III). Beyond calls for Steven Moffat to cast Sheppard in a role in *Sherlock* (to complete the trifecta), *SuperWhoLock* fans have used this actor's cross appearances to directly link the shows' diegesis. Fans have constructed *SuperWhoLock* texts that play on Sheppards' roles: Canton Delaware III from *Doctor Who* appearing in *Supernatural*, or Crowley talking to the Doctor.

Sheppard's presence in *Sherlock* would provide fodder for many fan fiction authors, *SuperWhoLock* or not. For Ashley Polasek, "Part of *Sherlock*'s unique appeal is that it provides an outlet for Holmes fans who wish to write yet don't feel themselves capable or willing to write for any other incarnation of the character"; that is, even though some *SuperWhoLock* (or even *WhoLock*) fan fiction might concentrate on the superficial or aesthetic similarities between the shows, much fan work revolves around the characters themselves.[43] But that does not mean that *Sherlock* fans are able—or even willing—to see *SuperWhoLock* become a canonized object. Both Ben and Pat, UK residents, are vehement about *SuperWhoLock* remaining outside the texts themselves. Pat thinks it would be OK to do "if they're going to do that … for a charity event, I think it could be real fun." Ben agrees, thinking that it would work "maybe if it was done as a one-off special, in an alternate universe but I wouldn't want to see it in the actual shows." Other *Sherlock* fans have different opinions. Yue, from China, knows about *Supernatural* and is a big fan of all three shows, but is "not a fan of fan fiction. They just rewrite the story, it's not very creative…the fan fiction they write… is too far from the show" (perhaps mirroring China's own policy on writers of fan fiction and slash).[44] In contrast, Tom, a fan from Germany, did not know too much about *SuperWhoLock* specifically, but was a big proponent of crossovers in general. He saw cosplay as a form of crossover text, and mixed his own cosplay from "*Doctor Who*, *Game of Thrones*, and stuff—mix it up to one outfit. Indiana Jones. I don't know—to feel like being in the series. So that's fandom—pretending or imagining or hoping that this is the universe that they're in."

Within *SuperWhoLock* fandom, though, Sherlock Holmes remains an important character. For Polasek, this is the power of *Sherlock* for the fan base:

> First, the show is different enough from its own source that writers can use it to explore themes that they would be less able to explore through the Canon. Second, in order to write about characters in a contemporary setting, fans need only have knowledge and experience of the world around them, rather than specific historical knowledge, to engage with the context of the show.[45]

In other words, fans need only develop an understanding of the character of Sherlock *within the diegesis of* Sherlock *the show* in order to create meaningful fan fiction; they do not have to deal with all the other representations of Sherlock Holmes throughout the ages. *Sherlock* flattens history and reinscribes the past with a retrofuturist aesthetic.[46] For *SuperWhoLock* fans, this means that although there are transmedia characteristics that guide the character Sherlock, there is enough mutability within those characteristics to provide ample opportunities for unique characterizations. In turn, the trans-fandom and inter-transmediated characteristics of *SuperWhoLock* reflect a similar characterization in the digital era.

Sherlocked Convention and the Fan Class System

To investigate *SuperWhoLock* fans within a *Sherlock* fandom, I attended the Sherlocked convention held in London at the ExCeL Centre in April 2015: interestingly, just a year and a half earlier, the ExCeL Centre had hosted the 50th anniversary celebration of *Doctor Who* and some of the people I interviewed at Sherlocked had attended that celebration.[47] The comparison to *Doctor Who* was on many people's minds at the Sherlocked convention, not just because of the shared space, but also because the two shows share a showrunner. Yet, the audiences for the two events were slightly different—beyond the fact the *Doctor Who* 50th anniversary was much larger and heavily attended—and UK resident Thom notes that this difference stems from the perceived audience of the two shows:

> I think *Sherlock* is a bit more adult oriented, as opposed to *Doctor Who*, which I think is more family orientated. So, I mean, looking at the crowd here [at Sherlocked], I'd say it's mostly people who are in their twenties and up. Not many people under teenage years, who sort of watch it and find it

> engaging. Whereas with something like *Doctor Who* young people can watch that and be hooked straight away.

The audience at Sherlocked was noticeably global: besides a couple of British people, in my interviews I spoke with people from France, Germany, Holland, the USA, and China, among others.

There were thousands of fans at *Sherlock*, and the show—despite having just nine episodes at the time of the convention (with a Christmas special having just been announced)—had proved popular enough with fans and critics to warrant the large event. Cumberbatch was undeniably a big draw for the fans at the convention: his presence was highly promoted in the run-up to the event, and even at the convention huge crowds followed him around (at one point, I saw him walk through a crowd and everyone parted in a tableau of religiosity).

The audience at Sherlocked was overwhelmingly female; although statistics have not been released (and my emails to the organizers have gone unanswered), I would estimate that more than three quarters of the attendees were women. Because of the popularity of Benedict Cumberbatch, there is an assumption that female fans of *Sherlock* are "only" fans because of Benedict Cumberbatch.[48] This assumption was repeated by some of the male fans I spoke with, including Ben who noted that in the *Sherlock* fandom:

> there're maybe people who aren't big into Sci-Fi, like the Drama and crime stories of *Sherlock* or vice versa. I think, as well, probably because of Benedict, there's been, obviously, the whole "Cumberbitch" fandom. Which I guess it must be flattering for Benedict. But at the same time they can be full on fandom. So I think a lot of them tend to be teenage, female fans.

"Cumberbitches" is a term, often used pejoratively, for female fans of Benedict Cumberbatch. Many of the women I spoke with, however, loathed the term and instead demonstrated a fandom of *Sherlock* and of Conan Doyle: Pat has been a Holmesian since she was 12, and was dismissive of the Cumberbatch fandom, supporting Busse's claim that fans internalize gendered constructions of "good" and "bad" fandom.[49] Other fans, like Nicole and her friends, go out of their way to show that they are fans of the entire Holmes experience:

> [We] go out to the Sherlock Holmes museum, and there was an exhibit shown at the London museum, Sherlock Holmes, we went to that. … I've

read all the books now. Support all the fans and the cast and the crew, and keep up to date with everything.

By far the most discussed aspect of the convention in my interviews was the cost of the tickets and the economics of being a fan. Adult ticket prices at Sherlocked ranged from a £29 single-day only ticket (for Saturday) to a £2995 VIP pass that included two autographs from each guest, two individual photos with each guest, and tickets to all the talks. Unlike the *Supernatural* convention or the *Doctor Who* convention, none of the talks were free for all ticket holders at Sherlocked—to hear Benedict Cumberbatch talk, for example, a single-day ticket holder would have to pay an additional £35, and to hear Andrew Scott (Moriarty), it would cost £20. The only free talk was the one with Steven Moffat and Mark Gatiss, although to get a ticket to that one, one had to also purchase a £20 ticket to hear either Lars Mikkelsen and Rupert Graves, or the "Ladies of Sherlock" panel. (Moffat's autograph was similarly free, perhaps because of the BBC's public service remit and his involvement with the organization of the convention—his production company, Hartswood Films, was a co-sponsor.) Individual photo shoots and autographs also cost money. For example, Cumberbatch's photo was £45, but he only signed autographs in person for people at the Platinum (£595) or VIP (£2995) level. Gold (£295) received a pre-signed photo in a "goodie bag," while the rest of us were out of luck. Other autographs ranged from free (Moffat and Sue Virtue) to £35 (Andrew Scott).

The topic of the economics of the convention was a popular one at Sherlocked, as fans often discussed people that had purchased a higher level than they had, or chatted about people with a lower priced package. There were five tiers of packages, each of which game slightly different benefits. The single-day (£29) provided a single-day ticket. The weekend pass (£44, which I had) gave the ticket holder access to the main hall on both Saturday and Sunday, as well as a special Friday evening opening. The Silver pass (£125) also provided the weekend access, and also five pre-assigned photo shoots (not selected by the ticket holder). The Gold pass (£295) provided all the above as well as one pre-signed autograph from Benedict Cumberbatch, five pre-assigned autographs (not selected by the ticket holder), one photo with each guest, and one ticket to a talk with each guest. The Platinum pass (£595) provided all the above as well as the chance to have Cumberbatch sign in person and additional photos. The

VIP pass (£2995) provided all the above as well as additional photographs, autographs, talks, and access to complimentary refreshments.

The different economic levels and pass attributes created a class system within the fan environment of Sherlocked. By "class system," I am referring here to the sense of economic value that is brought to bear in fan hierarchies. As a subcultural system, fandom has been viewed as a cultural economy and a knowledge hierarchy; and issues of taste and social class undergird many of the dialogues about fan distinctiveness.[50] For Pat, the entire Holmes fandom is classist in terms of subcultural knowledge capital, as different fans will have more or less knowledge competency about the original canon. Sandvoss notes that fan studies have used the work of Bourdieu to "unmask… forms of judgment based on authenticity and originality…as means of social and cultural distinction."[51] In other words, fan studies that use Bourdieu as a theoretical model examine the class markers that govern the types of texts people are fans of, the ways of engaging with those texts, and the interactions of the different fan communities as constitutive of fandom itself.[52] The earliest days of fan studies, including the canonical work of John Fiske, show how "the cultural system works like the economic system to distribute its recourses unequally and thus to distinguish between the privileged and the deprived."[53] Culture and economy become linked via fan cultures.

Sherlocked exemplified this cultural system; in fact, beyond *working like* an economic system, the convention seemed to turn a cultural system into a literal economic one. The result of this is that Sherlocked created an ideology of economic classism for attendees. The British class system is perhaps one of the clearest examples of social hierarchy throughout history; from sociological reports to classic cultural studies investigations in the mid-twentieth century, British classism has been the subject of numerous cultural, sociological, economic, and political studies.[54] These studies and examinations of class culture persist today: in a recent article about *Doctor Who*, Ninth Doctor Christopher Eccleston argued that "inequality is still rife in British society, with the rise of privileged actors" using upper-class accepts (he used a Northern accept for the Doctor, representing a more working-class background). In his interview, Eccleston mentioned Cumberbatch as an example of this "milky, anodyne" culture, and the upper-class hierarchies present within British acting.[55] It is thus perhaps unsurprising that that most British of all fan heroes, Sherlock Holmes, should be the instigator of an economic class system within fandom.

Perhaps one of the clearest examples of this ideology of classism occurred while I was standing in line waiting to get into the show. Each of the different tiers had their own lines (Platinum and Gold shared a line, as did Silver and Weekend). Here, fanqueue culture is on full display, as we not only lined up to get into the show, but also lined up within the show for autographs, for photos, for the panel, and for entrance into the main store. The queue on left side of the hall was the VIPs; after those 200+ (by my count) people entered the main hall, the Platinum and Gold shared the next line, the Silver and Weekend the line on the right side of the hall, with the single-day-only pass holders all the way on the far side of the room.

In my line I stood behind three women who had purchased Silver passes. One woman turned behind her to look at the single-day-only pass holders and said to her friends, rather dismissively, "I can't believe they couldn't even spend the extra few pounds to get the weekend rate!" She then, a few minutes later, looked at the Gold package holders, in line in front of her, and exclaimed, "I can't believe anyone would want to spend 300 pounds to get into this event." The confluence of economics, class, and taste is drawn clearly here: people who spend less than she did were not as serious a fan as she was, and people who spent more were frivolous and not careful with their money.

The fans I spoke with were divided on how the economics of the convention created a hierarchy, however. Thom, who bought the Platinum package for £595, thought that, at first:

> some people weren't very happy about it—the price was a factor, the way it was set out, things like that. But I think, to be honest with you, people who really enjoy it, look at it as it might be a one off experience. Then some people are prepared to pay that bit of money, and meet the actors and see how the show that we love and hold to our hearts hold together. ... is it worth spending 600 pounds to meet these people? ... I probably wouldn't do it again, [but] I thought I'd go for it, I have a spare bit of money, just thought I'd take a chance on it.

Other fans, like Tayna, weighed the options carefully:

> I looked at the different prices and I could've afforded Silver, barely, but I thought I'm not sure if Silver's actually a package worthwhile buying. I think Gold and up is where you get enough benefits to make it worth it, and it was 300 pounds and I had to…I think I didn't have enough money on my card when they went on sale, and I kept looking at all my cards and trans-

> ferring money into the same account—two pounds there and five pounds there, and I only had enough for a weekend ticket.

There is a discourse of worth and value being discussed at this convention: the worth and value of the *fan* is translated into the worth and value of how much *money* the fan has to get into the event. Not only does this contrast with views of fandom as a homogenous community, it also contrasts with the inter-connectedness demonstrated by *SuperWhoLock* fandom. Whereas *SuperWhoLock* fans use their multiple fandoms to construct one massive crossover text, the fans at Sherlocked were artificially divided: kept in different queues, given different packages and even different badges, the different tiers created a separation of fan engagement.

Many fans were unaware that the convention was a corporate affair. For example, Tom, who purchased a Silver package, thought if

> it was just a BBC thing, then it would be just for the fans. And not just the fans being a money machine, which they are now with all the categories and I can understand there being a VIP package or something, but all these "silver, gold, platinum, normal"—that's a bit odd.

Sarah pays "shit tons of money to come to things like this" but would rather go online to Tumblr to show her fan spirit. She did not think there was a classist hierarchy at play at Sherlocked, but then contradicted herself, as she remarked that the different levels of ticket prices demonstrate "different level[s] of commitment and passion" in the fan community.

The economic classism of Sherlocked rubbed off on the fan community in other ways. Once entry into the main hall was secure, some activities were scattered around: a visual effects show, a free stage with limited seating that including fan-run panels like "cosplay on a budget" and "the fashion of Sherlock." Promoted panels on the free stage included the "premiere" of *Sherlock: The Network*, a mobile app game. There was a small "museum" with fashion from the show, a number of stalls selling authorized merchandise (as far as I could see, there was just one booth advertising fan cosplay products), and various large props (a bus, for example) scattered around. Two sets had been reconstructed for viewing: the main 221B Baker Street set, and the office of Mycroft Holmes. Both were available for photo ops. For the most part, fanqueue culture was highly visible. Queuing seemed to be the main attraction: one would stand in line for autographs (if you had paid for them), stand in line for photo ops (again, if you had paid for them), stand in line to have your photo taken in front of the main door at 221B Baker Street, or queue for the main BBC *Sherlock* shop (Fig. 4.3).

In many ways, despite the hierarchies and class systems built into the event, the fans at Sherlocked were happy and engaged. There was a spirit of conviviality at Sherlocked that matched the feelings at Gallifrey One and the *Supernatural* convention. Tanya, a fan I interviewed, thought this was less because of the celebrities and more because these are fans who do not normally get together in physical locations:

> In more Western fandoms… there's quite a bit of distance between the actual performers (the actors who make the show) and the fans. It's very difficult to get in touch; even [photo ops] … is not even an interaction, it's three words. And the people who pay thousands of pounds to get VIP tickets, and I'm thinking, you don't really get in touch with the people unless you have money or connections. So it's mostly about connecting with other fans and just sharing things you like—fan fiction, pictures—and it's more about the fan community than it is about the actual thing you're a fan of.

Vidalie, who had traveled across the English Channel to the convention, thought it was "magical" to connect with other fans, as "every fandom is a

Fig. 4.3 Queue to fanqueue: the line for the BBC *Sherlock* shop (Photo by the author)

community—with codes, with references, with cosplay, and thought.... It's where there's a shared [vision] with the author." Jessica found Sherlocked "a very welcoming community and it's a really friendly place to be."

At a moment in time when fandom is becoming more mainstream (and fan activities are appropriated by media corporations),[56] it is telling that, as Faye describes, "the ever-shifting world of electronic communication and Internet technology have ... altered the face of Sherlockian culture, allowing enthusiasts without the desire to travel for meetings nevertheless to engage in meaningful social dialogue and creative effort revolving around their hero."[57] For many fans who were unable to attend (or afford) the ticket prices for Sherlocked, the Internet—and Tumblr culture more specifically—opened up avenues to participate with (or rally against) the commercial convention. The "Unlocked: The Official Sherlock PJ Party" was an online convention organized by a number of *Sherlock* fans on Tumblr.[58] Billed as "an alternative activity for fans who can't go to Sherlocked, but still want to spend the weekend having fun talking about their favorite show," the event encouraged free and open fan-run discussion during the three days that Sherlocked ran. Events included real-time panel discussions held in text-based chat rooms, watchalong marathons of episodes, advice for writing *Sherlock* fan fiction, discussion over the autism spectrum (related to Sherlock Holmes himself), fan work challenges, and many other panels, quizzes, workshops, and discussions—all held online and all held in comparison to Sherlocked. Altogether, the panels totaled over 671 text pages of transcribed discussion and interaction.

Although a fan-run event, the Unlocked convention only existed because the Sherlocked convention created an economic hierarchy within the world of *Sherlock* fandom. Unlocked was specifically billed as something for people who *could not* attend—inscribing Sherlocked with the veneer of officiality and authorization over the fandom. Like the fans I spoke with, Sherlocked was *the event*, and to have been a part of it was to demonstrate a true fan experience. Thus, the fans that attended also became part of the very classist ideology that undergirds other fan communities, and reveals a hierarchy at the heart of multiple fan communities—the topic for the final chapter of this book.

Conclusion

According to Stein and Busse, writing here about the way *Sherlock* embraces multiplicity: "even if we can't agree whether *Sherlock* has fully been successful in its 21st century adaptation, we can agree that fandom in all its myriad affirmative and transformative creativity has taken this modern Sherlock and made him fully and unapologetically postmodern, and in the process he has become a shared entity, potent in his very multiplicity."[59] *SuperWhoLock* exemplifies their discussion of the postmodern version of Sherlock—much like it exemplifies similar roles for the Doctor and for the Winchester brothers.

Fans of *Sherlock* at Sherlocked respond both to the show and to the multiple ways the character manifests throughout his various iterations. Nicole, a fan at Sherlocked, told me that with "*Sherlock* it's different because we're all separated … there is so much to explore and think about, that everyone has different opinions." But while "that separates [the fandom] … there's still a whole collective of 'you like *Sherlock*, I like *Sherlock* too, we'll be friends' at the convention." *SuperWhoLock*, although dependent upon the Cumberbatch portrayal of the detective, allows for this multiplicity in the different attributes given to him. As Lamerichs describes, "viewers [of *Sherlock*] have a wide range of repertoires that guide them in their readings. Though transmedial elements form cues for audiences, they often bridge these with other experiences and fiction. Aside from alluding to other versions of *Sherlock Holmes*, viewers rely on their own experiences, knowledge of popular culture and literature."[60] The mainstreaming of fandom also reveals that viewers can rely on *other fandoms*: Tumblr and other outlets make *SuperWhoLock* engaging for readers and viewers of *Sherlock* by presenting these multiple views in one outlet.

Sherlock (in *Sherlock*) is not free of industrial and corporate construction—and yet Lindsay Faye describes *Sherlock* fandom as "a living culture as much as it is a repository for creative effort, highly focused on participatory commentary and meritocratic feedback, and thus to conflate the democracy of fandom with pecuniary pastiche marketing would be injudicious and offensive."[61] The corporate function of Sherlock manifests most directly in the engagement with the fan audience at Sherlocked. The cultural capital of *Sherlock* fans, used in *SuperWhoLock* as a way of binding together the inter-transmediated dimensions of the crossover text, was enacted through economic means and mechanisms at the Sherlocked convention. Fandom, both an economic force and a communal glue, creates different expectations from corporate creators; the existence of *SuperWhoLock*, however, reveals an outlet for fans' engagement even within the structure of class hierarchies. Not just a mechanism for creativity, *SuperWhoLock* is a revelation of the way fans' multiple concerns can be reflected in a single text. The crossover of *SuperWhoLock* is not just a crossover of text, it is a crossover of fan engagement.

Notes

1. Porter, *Doctor Who Franchise*.
2. Jamison, *Fic*.
3. Basu, "Sherlock," 208.
4. Pearson, "Bachies, Bardies, Trekkies, and Sherlockians," 105; see also Pearson, "'It's Always 1895,'" 148–9.
5. Hills, "Epistemological Economy," 32.
6. Jensen, "Fandom as Pathology," 9.
7. Hills, *Fan Cultures*, 47–8.
8. Pearson, "Bachies, Bardies, Trekkies, and Sherlockians," 99.
9. Hills, *Fan Cultures*, 49.
10. Hills, "'Twilight' Fans"; Pearson, "Bachies, Bardies, Trekkies, and Sherlockians."
11. Stein and Busse, "Introduction," 11.
12. Bochman, "*Sherlock Holmes*," 1.
13. Booth, *Playing Fans*, 30.
14. Hills, *Fan Cultures*.
15. Hills, "Epistemological Economy," 37–8.
16. Coppa, "Sherlock as Cyborg"; Hills, "Epistemological Economy," 31.
17. Booth, *Playing Fans*.
18. Hills, "Epistemological Economy."
19. Sandvoss, *Fans*.
20. Evans, "Shaping Sherlocks."
21. Porter, *Doctor Who Franchise*, 10.
22. Faye, "Prologue," 5.
23. Stein and Busse, "Introduction"; Jamison, *Fic*.
24. Stein and Busse, "Introduction," 15.
25. Polasek, "Winning," 49.
26. Polasek, "Winning," 53; Sheehan, "Queer-baiting"; see also Lavigne, "Noble Bachelor," 14.
27. Taylor, "Holmesian Shapeshifting."
28. Coppa, "Sherlock as Cyborg," 210.
29. Stein and Busse, "Introduction," 10.
30. Jenkins, *Convergence Culture*, 14.
31. Busse and Stein, "Conclusion," 227.
32. Hills, "Epistemological Economy," 29.
33. Coppa, "Sherlock as Cyborg"; Hills, "Epistemological Economy."
34. Briggs, commentary.
35. Needless Procedures.
36. Booth, *Playing Fans*; also, Zubernis and Larsen, *Fandom at the Crossroads*; Tosenberger; Felschow, "Hey, Check it Out"; Wilkinson, "A Box of Mirrors."

37. Harvey, "Sherlock's Webs," 123.
38. Chapman, Inside the *TARDIS*, 78.
39. Harvey, "Sherlock's Webs," 118.
40. Smith. "WhoLock."
41. Hibbard, "Doctor Who Movie."
42. Perez, "Gif Fics."
43. Polasek, "Winning," 51.
44. Romano, "Chinese Authorities."
45. Polasek, "Winning," 52.
46. Basu, "Sherlock."
47. Hills, *Unfolding Event.*
48. Porter, Benedict Cumberbatch; a female fan stereotype discussed by Busse, "Geek Hierarchies"; also Jensen, "Fandom as Pathology."
49. Busse, "Geek Hierarchies."
50. Fiske, "Cultural Economy; Hills, Fan Cultures; Jenkins, *Convergence Culture*; Busse, "Geek Hierarchies"; Bourdieu, *Distinction.*
51. Sandvoss, "Death of the Reader," 27.
52. Hills, *Fan Cultures*, 46–55.
53. Fiske, "Cultural Economy," 31.
54. See Goldthorpe and Lockwood, "Affluence."
55. Doran, "Christopher Eccleston."
56. Booth, *Playing Fans.*
57. Faye, "Prologue," 6.
58. unlockedcon.tumblr.com.
59. Stein and Busse, "Introduction," 23.
60. Lamerichs, "Holmes Abroad," 192.
61. Faye, "Prologue," 3.

CHAPTER 5

Conclusion: *SuperWhoLock* Fandom: Cross Fandoms

Abstract This conclusion to *Crossing Fandoms* explores the *SuperWhoLock* crossover as a metaphor for heterogeneous fan cultures. The chapter examines fan antagonism and fan affect. The flattening of affect in the digital age seemingly negates the difference between fan groups, but *SuperWhoLock* reveals tensions at the heart of fan culture. *SuperWhoLock* presents an unusual case where the antagonism is neither completely directed ***outside*** the text nor completely directed ***inside*** the fandom. Rather, *SuperWhoLock* antagonism emerges from the tension between the non-canon aspects of the corpus and the requisite fan experiences of the original three texts.

Keywords *SuperWhoLock* • Fan antagonism • Anti-fandom • Tensions • Digital fandom

In this book, I have been exploring the way fans have come together, melded their ideas, and created a new, unstable, crossover fiction. *SuperWhoLock* is undoubtedly a fan-made text, but it is also a metaphor for the larger changes occurring in our digital media environment: the coming together of cult media, fandom, and narrative originality presents a view of the flexible, in-process nature of contemporary media. Using the metaphor of the fan convention, I have examined spaces of fandom

P. Booth, *Crossing Fandoms*, DOI 10.1057/978-1-137-57455-8_5

as epicenters of fan identity; I have examined the crossover between fan groups as a way of focusing on the cultural phenomenon of *SuperWhoLock*.

SuperWhoLock is not the only crossover text that has ever existed—far from it. As Henry Jenkins described in *Textual Poachers*, crossover texts are one of the ten ways that fans can rewrite media texts—and he focuses specifically on one of the core elements of *SuperWhoLock*, *Doctor Who*:

> "Cross-over" stories blur the boundaries between different texts. …Some series forms (*Doctor Who*, *Quantum Leap*) lend themselves particularly well to cross-overs, since the primary texts already involve a constant dislocation for the protagonists. The TARDIS has materialized every place from the Planet of the Apes to Fawlty Towers, even on the set of *Wheel of Fortune*… "Cross-over" stories break down not only the boundaries between texts but also those between genres, suggesting how familiar characters might function in radically different environments.[1]

In this final chapter, I want to explore what Jenkins mentions here, the "radically different environments" of the crossover, not wholly as aspects of *SuperWhoLock* as a corpus of texts—although *SuperWhoLock*'s dissonance, as I will discuss, is as important as its resonance—but rather as a way of looking at the heterogeneous fandom of *SuperWhoLock* and fans' relationships to each other. That is, the radically different environment I am interested in is not necessarily the one that places the TARDIS next to Vanna White, or has Sam Beckett leaping into the body of Captain Jonathan Archer, but rather the environment of fan affect, and *SuperWhoLock*'s "radically different" affect.

Fan antagonism has always been a part of fan audiences.[2] Stanfill notes how two bodies of fan stereotyping exist: the first is based on mainstream notions of *how* to be a fan and the second is based on stereotypes *about* being a fan.[3] Dare-Edwards similarly describes different modes of fan antagonism: inter-fandom antagonism takes place between disparate fan groups, while intra-fandom antagonism takes place by fans of the same object.[4] Yet, the flattening of affect in the digital age negates the difference between inter- and intra-fan antagonisms. That is, as mediation becomes more ubiquitous, the distinction between inter-fan arguments and intra-fan discussion is diminished. *SuperWhoLock* presents an unusual case where the antagonism is neither completely directed *outside* the text nor completely directed *inside* the fandom. Rather, *SuperWhoLock* antagonism emerges from the tension between the non-canon aspects of the corpus and the requisite fan experiences of the original three texts.

SuperWhoLock is necessarily about the parts of *Supernatural*, *Doctor Who*, and *Sherlock* that match—the Moffat connection, the "madman" (with or without a box) connection, the Amy Pond connection, the supernatural beast connection, or even the (Falling/Weeping) Angels connection (Fig. 5.1).

As I have detailed in this book, fans have picked up on these semantic connections to create "syntactic reproduction[s] of ideological moments from a media text…[representing] a liminal state between fandom and media industry."[5] In this way, I have focused on the similarities between

Fig. 5.1 Connections between aspects of *SuperWhoLock*, by 924inlegend (http://924inlegend.tumblr.com/post/54015648110/superwholock-angels)

the fan groups as well, both from semantic and syntactic points of view. With that in mind, I have been exploring the points of connection, the compatibility, and complementary natures of fans of *Supernatural*, Whovians, and Sherlockians. Think of *SuperWhoLock* as a Venn diagram, where the overlaps between the three shows reveal complementary information. But a key aspect of a Venn diagram is what is left *out* of the overlap, not necessarily that which makes it up. To place one particular image of *SuperWhoLock* within the pantheon of disconnected other images of *SuperWhoLock*, along with any continuities with *Supernatural*, *Doctor Who*, and *Sherlock*, is to necessarily invite discontinuities. In Fig. 5.1, the referent for "angel" is vastly different between the three texts. In *Supernatural*, Castiel is referring to the Biblical Angels, warriors of God, that fight a battle with demons (and eventually humankind). In *Doctor Who*, the Weeping Angels are aliens, so named because they take the form of angelic statues whenever they are observed. There is nothing biblical about them (despite their appearance; they could just as easily be the Weeping Politicians, if they took the shapes of political statues), and in the universe of *Doctor Who*, nothing supernatural. The Angels reference in *Sherlock* is even more oblique—rather than referring to actual entities, Moriarty references Sherlock's ultimate "good"-ness and his metaphorical connection to "angels" as symbols of peace.

Thus, while there is a semantic connection between these shows which *SuperWhoLock* ably picks up on, *SuperWhoLock* is equally about the differences between the shows. That this example of the Angel uses Castiel rather than Gabriel or David Tennant's Tenth Doctor rather Peter Capaldi's Twelfth indicates that there is a choice to be made in the placement of *SuperWhoLock* elements; and whenever there is a choice in fan communities, no matter how symbiotic they might be, there will be disagreement. As Polasek argues: "The act of interpreting a text affects future readings of that text; therefore, creating an onscreen interpretation not only involves the action of the source on the film, but also an action of the film on the source."[6] For fans of *Sherlock*, *Supernatural*, or *Doctor Who*, reacting to and creating *SuperWhoLock* images means making a choice about interpretation and acting upon the source text in some way: creating a meaning and concretizing that meaning in the relationship between semantic moments.

For *SuperWhoLock*, disagreement does not necessarily mean discontinuity. In fact, it is in the places of rupture *between* the *Supernatural*, the *Doctor Who*, and the *Sherlock* that fans (and fan researchers) can explore the larger context of the *SuperWhoLock* phenomenon. For many fans, disagreement is "an outlet to express themselves about things they cared about and often a way to analyze themselves by identifying with and deconstructing or exploring a character or ideas in the text. It was also incredibly important to them to have found a community of like-minded people with whom to engage in this process without being shamed or mocked."[7] At the same time, *SuperWhoLock* fans are not always so understanding of different viewpoints.

In this chapter, I explore the non-harmonious relationship between *SuperWhoLock* fans of *Supernatural*, *Doctor Who*, and *Sherlock* to investigate differences, stereotypes, and animosities in fan communities. The fans I spoke with at the Gallifrey One convention, the *Supernatural* convention, and the Sherlocked convention had different opinions and ideas about the *other* fans that make up the *SuperWhoLock* fan communities. Using *SuperWhoLock* as a metaphor of fan cultures in the digital age means seeing beyond the commonalities and into the dark heart of fan antagonism.[8]

Fan Antagonism

The notion that groups of fans are not harmonious is not new, although as Mel Stanfill points out, "By comparison to the volume of analysis on other aspects of fandom such as transformative production practices (fan fiction and/or vidding) or community organization ... the number of scholars engaging in this work is conspicuously small."[9] Kristina Busse describes how groups of fans will always mock those that are lower on the social order than they are: no matter where "one is situated in terms of mockable fannish behavior, there is clearly a fannish subgroup even more extreme than one's own, and it is that group that one can feel secure in not being a part of."[10] Stanfill's research on *Xena* fans reveals that more than just the text is mockable here: "These patterns in intra-fandom stigmatization suggest that higher socioeconomic status, more intense involvement in the fan world, or a combination of the two leads to a more strongly felt need to stave off culturally devalued ideas about fans."[11] Mockery is a class-based activity, as discussed in Chap. 4, and fandom can bring class-based hierarchies. For Hills, fan "stereotyping is profoundly ironic, as it suggests that fan cultures who may themselves historically have been victims of pathologizing stereotypes...are now in some instances turning those patterns of stereotyping onto other, younger fans and fandoms."[12] When faced with stigmatization by mainstream culture, fans both reflect and deflect those concerns onto more devalued types of fans. *SuperWhoLock* is no different. As I mentioned in the Introduction, rarely does one come directly to *SuperWhoLock* as a main fan text: instead, the traditional route is to be part of a fan community already, or to be a fan of one (or more) of the three particular shows, and to be drawn into the *SuperWhoLock* fandom via that show. The three points of entry into the crossover text reveal a morphological reading of fandom: often, fans' viewpoints on the unfolding of *SuperWhoLock* depend on the originating text from which they came.

In his assessment of inter-fandom antagonism toward *Twilight* fans from (among others) *Buffy the Vampire Slayer* fans, Matt Hills argues that the "fan cultures pathologized ... one another" and in "more contingently and in diverse ways across fan communities." Devaluing *Twilight* fans as overly sexualized and "creepy," the *Buffy* fans, as well as fans at Comic-Con, created "inter-fandom pathologization," where one fan group acts antagonistically toward another.[13] Looking more closely at fan antagonism, Helena Dare-Edwards differentiates between inter-fandom and intra-fandom antagonisms in *iCarly* fan circles: 'inter-fandom usually refers to disparate fan groups ... [while] an inter-fandom dynamic [examines] ... fans of the same object but in different spaces.'[14]

In some of my interviews, *SuperWhoLock* fans mentioned similar types of inter- and intra-antagonistic behavior at some conventions. For instance, Lindsey, an attendee at the Creation Entertainment *Supernatural* convention, mentioned that she had previously gone to Leakycon:

> There was a group of four girls, and they were like "hey join us because you're by yourself" ...And we were talking about *The Vampire Diaries* and they were like, "Are you about Stefan or Damon?" and I was like "Oh totally Damon" and they were like "Ugh! You can't be with us anymore—you have to leave, you can't be in our group "anymore"...They were like, we can't be together because we're totally different, because you like the different guy.

Many of the analyses of the inter-antagonistic fan relate the concept to the anti-fan, the "opposite" of the traditional fan who "hate[s] or dislike[s] a given text, personality, or genre."[15] Antagonism and dislike seem to exist as similar feelings, and the actions of anti-fans seem like those of antagonistic fans.[16] Bethan Jones's analysis of Brony fandom—male fans of the show *My Little Pony: Friendship is Magic*—outlines the difference between anti-fandom of a *text* and anti-fandom of a *fandom*:

> Much work on anti-fandom has focused on the concept of 'bad texts', that is, the text itself being deserving of criticism, dislike and even hate because it is badly written, lacking in literary merit or problematic in the sexual, racial or gender politics it expresses… Brony anti-fandom, in contrast, is focused upon the fans of the text, rather than the text itself.[17]

That being said, anti-fandom and antagonistic fandom are different. Hills begins his analysis of inter-fandom antagonism by looking specifically at cases of anti-fandom; that is, when one audience rejects another. Hills argues, however, that instead of "anti-fandom," with its sports-rivalry mentality, does not apply as readily to media texts where "one fan culture defines itself against and negatively stereotypes another." "This is not quite 'anti-fandom' he argues, but is rather a kind of fan protectionism, and boundary-maintenance." Rather than anti-fandom, he argues for a theory of antagonisms which "moves beyond the conceptual frame of anti-fandom, operating as a more contested, contingent, and multiple set of readings."[18] Similarly, Rebecca Williams notes, in her analysis of Muse fans and *Twilight* fans, "Since there is no clear reason for Muse and Twilight fans to be in opposition to each other here—apart from Muse's "accidental" connection to the saga—[the] conception of anti-fandom does not fully apply."[19]

Fan antagonism, meanwhile, illustrates the points of rupture or disagreement between fans as entry points into understanding the construction of the loved text. Karkanias's research into the ruptures within *Supernatural* fandom is relevant here. She splits *Supernatural* fans into different "camps" (Sam Girls, Dean Girls, Brothers Fans, Wincest Fans, Castiel [Cas] Girls, Destiel Fans, Anti-Fans, Extreme Sam Girls, Extreme Dean Fans), and illustrates how each camp feels about the others. She lumps "girls" and "Fans" semantically together. She finds that, for example, "Dean Girls and Extreme Sam Girls find themselves at odds with each other over the content of their interpretations, but looking at their arguments reveals they also conflict with each other over the correct way to derive an interpretation from the show." Karkanias illustrates the inter-fandom arguments "as each party often feels personally attacked when their interpretation is being picked apart, because they often identify so closely with it."[20] Karkanias's article reflects much of what Lynn Zubernis and Katherine Larsen discovered about the "bullying, conflict and aggression" within *Supernatural* fandoms.[21] They relate the antagonism of "intra-fandom" groups to a psychological need to police the boundaries of the groups to which fans belong[22]: "we still retain our intense fear of being excluded…[so] people react with what on the surface may appear to be an out of proportion response."[23] Rob, one of the people I interviewed at Gallifrey One, noted a similar feeling, putting it like this: "So this type of fan culture, you're very protective of what you're a fan of, because you identify so much with it."

Both for Zubernis and Larson and for Karkanias, one key nexus point around which fans argued was canon—an interpretation of what is officially part of the text and what is not. While few arguments center on the *depiction* of events in the *Supernatural* corpus, there are numerous discussions and disagreements about the *meaning* of these events. "It's canon" can apply to both the events and the meaning of the events:

> Fans speak … over each other or criticize … each other's conclusions without fully understanding how the other reached these conclusions or how they are using the text.[24]

Within fannish circles, adherence to a particular canon is one of the most important precepts.[25]

Clearly, antagonism and anti-fandom are linked, but in the case of *SuperWhoLock*, there are additional differences between anti-fan and antagonistic fan. In other words, inter-fandom moves between fan objects while intra-fandom delves into one fan object deeply. But *SuperWhoLock* is not one text but rather a corpus of texts, and fans of *SuperWhoLock* are *also* fans of at least some of the requisite three texts. So antagonism is neither completely *inter-fandom* or *intra-fandom* as the text itself is neither completely whole nor completely disparate. It is, in fact, a completely *digital* fandom, symbolic of the ubiquity of mediation and interface in contemporary fandom. Fans are *not* just uni-fannish, and their fan affect will necessarily be fluid across multiple fan groups and fannish objects. As my interviewee Cinnamon Hayes said, "we definitely can be polygamous in our fandom." So when a fan is antagonistic toward a fellow *SuperWhoLock* fan, she is rarely antagonist toward the *text* as there is not a central canon about which fans can argue and debate; or, rather, no one construction of a canon for *SuperWhoLock* can be considered any more authoritative than any other one. Interestingly, very few fans were antagonistic at all toward *SuperWhoLock* the text during out interviews: it was only when I mentioned that I was writing a book about it that there seemed to be incredulity, as if they were asking why these fans were more interesting than others. The sentiment seemed to be condemning fans "as people" instead as of fans.[26]

There are two types of antagonistic fans related to *SuperWhoLock*. The first are people that are fans of *Sherlock*, *Doctor Who*, or *Supernatural* but do not see the relevance or point of combining them. In my conversations with fans, this was only stated a few times, but those fans were quite adamant. We might call this type of anti-fandom of *SuperWhoLock* in general. For instance, Anna Marie, a fan of *Doctor Who*, simply finds *SuperWhoLock* "amusing to be seen." Nicole, who had been a fan of *SuperWhoLock*, became tired of mashing up her three favorite shows, and wanted "to keep them separate, for [her] own reasons." Similarly, Sarah does not understand why people would combine shows like that, "because in [her] head they're all in distinct little universes and ...[the] only amount of crossover [she] can handle is the Marvel world." Jennifer added "I don't understand why it's just those three... What's the connection with those three?" Sarah did not like the way the British shows and the American did not quite fit together; like Nicole, she wanted to keep them separate. Tanya wanted to ignore *SuperWhoLock* because she did not have enough time to devote to it: "There's not enough space in my life for three fandoms, I just have to watch the one." But perhaps the clearest anti-fandom for *SuperWhoLock* came from Yue, who told me that people who write fan fiction *in general* were "not very creative" and "crazy."

A second type of antagonism in *SuperWhoLock* fandom is where fans of the requisite texts look down on or pre-judge other fans of the requisite texts. In other words, while *SuperWhoLock* may unite fans as a corpus, the mechanism by which *SuperWhoLock* is constructed reveals schisms in fan relations. Much like the inter-fandom antagonism described by Hills, fans of *Sherlock* may disregard *Doctor Who* fans or *Supernatural* fans, or any combination thereof.[27] Williams describes how "interloping fans," or fans that have latched onto one text because of its relation to another text, "have been devalued and seen as inauthentic, and ... this relates to common lines of division within fan cultures which make distinctions based on age, experience, longevity of fandom, and gender."[28] Perhaps more common than any other type of antagonism, this interloping fan antagonism is present in *SuperWhoLock* fandom because of the unique entry points into *SuperWhoLock*.

Although *Supernatural*, *Doctor Who*, and *Sherlock* are all cult texts, they do also all have different cultural connotations (about quality, about longevity, about cultural value, about heritage, about nationalism). The differences between the cultural value of these "cult" texts with passionate and related fan audiences hearken toward the antagonism that Hills and Williams describe of *Twilight*, Jones describes of *My Little Pony*, or Harman and Jones describe of *Fifty Shades of Grey*.[29] For example, Juliet,[30] a *Doctor Who* fan, replicates many of the same pathological discourses about *Supernatural* fans that Stanfill notes of *Xena* fans' inter-fandom antagonisms. The fans that Stanfill interviewed "shared some of the larger culture's standards of proper media interaction, had a sense of fan behavior as potentially inappropriate, and even believed many anti-fan stereotypes to be accurate." These fans had a "dual vision," seeing fandom both "as fans and as non-fans looking at fans through a mainstream, stereotyped lens": for example, they would refer to what they saw as *other* fans' "unreasonable consumerism"; their devotion to "the cultivation of worthless knowledge"; their being "out of touch with reality"; and their "emotionally and intellectually immature" nature.[31] Juliet, after seeing *Sherlock* fans at an event, noted that "they're very much … younger than I am and kinda crazy… For them it's almost religious, it's almost as if [*Sherlock*] is their church, it's the one thing they can go to and feel safe and do all sorts of things they won't normally do if they're not with other fans. And so I don't know what's it's about." Further, despite never going to a *Supernatural* event, Juliet also notes that the *Supernatural* fandom seems "kind of crazy." Another fan, Cinnamon, compared her *Doctor Who* and *Star Trek* fandoms to Marvel fandom: "Some of the more superhero ones … They tend to be more into guns, and more versed as far as that goes. But I think there's a slightly socially liberal tilt to *Doctor Who* and *Star Trek*." Here, the fan audiences are judged by the texts they are passionate about, clearly replicating the pathologization that Jenkins describes in early fan studies and Stanfill perceives in contemporary fan audiences. At the *Supernatural* convention, Jennifer revealed her own implicit antagonism toward those who were not dressed as (what she would consider) appropriate cosplay. When two *Dr. Horrible* cosplayers came walking by, Jennifer noted that she just did not "get it":

> I don't get why we're cosplaying something other than *Supernatural*.... I have such a hard time getting into *Doctor Who*, but I love *Sherlock* and I love *Supernatural* more than the other two. But I guess in my mind, I think—and this might be where I sound stuck up? —but I'm like, we're here for *Supernatural*. ... To see people cosplaying as anything other than *Supernatural* is hard because we're really here to bond over *Supernatural*.

This antagonism within *SuperWhoLock* fan communities reveals the influence of the mainstreaming of fandom on contemporary fan audiences. I have previously written about the way fans are subtly disciplined into creating artificial boundaries on fan affect by the depiction of "hyperfans" on television and in film (a hyperfan is an overt, stereotypical display of fandom, usually negatively perceived).[32] For the fans I interviewed, there were *fans* and then there were *obsessive or overt fans*—always somewhere else, and always giving fandom a bad name. For example, Rob subtly mocks the passion (and what he perceives as the ignorance) of *Sherlock* fans: "[They're] Tweeting obsessively, 'Oh I can't believe Sherlock is still alive' Even though you should've read the books even though they would've told you he didn't die, but whatever." Delilah[33] also takes umbrage with the *Sherlock* fans, both as they are in infancy and because they seem obsessed with Benedict Cumberbatch:

> From the little I see of *Sherlock* [fandom], I can only say that when I see the cosplaying it seems to be very typical. ... I haven't seen a lot of the same creativity as I have with the *Doctor Who* fandom as far as people doing their own audios, their own fan movies, their own versions of cosplay. At the same time the *Sherlock* fandom as we know it based on the show isn't as old as *Doctor Who* fandom. So in my mind the TV show *Sherlock* fandom is still in its infancy. And I think the people that like *Doctor Who* and the people that like *Sherlock*, are both in my opinion are drawn in because of the intellectual perspective.

Interestingly, Delilah's argument is echoed by Hills' discussion of the way *Twilight* fans were pathologized as being in a "feral" fandom, or what he calls a "threshold" fandom—a fandom that is nascent and devalued, but will eventually (the assumption goes) "grow up" into a more "refined" fan object (e.g., graduating from *Twilight* to *Buffy* or from *Doctor Who* to *Sherlock*).[34]

Amy decries the *Doctor Who* fandom—even though she would consider herself a fan of *Doctor Who*—as being difficult and insular. She notes that

"Even if you've only watched the new series like I have, it doesn't feel like you're completely part of that fandom because there are still those pieces you're missing." Lucie, another fan I interviewed at Sherlocked, agreed with Amy, saying that "*Doctor Who* fans can be really old because the show is really old. Whereas *Sherlock* fans are emotionally…young." At the same time, Jonathan separates

> the casual fan, someone's who's aware of it, and someone who's a fan. … Some people take it more seriously, some people are more hard about it, other people just follow it here or there. I have friends who, every week *Doctor Who*'s on, they'll watch it—religiously—they'll watch an episode three or four times. I have other friends who catch up on the series on Netflix half a year later. I have other friends who wait until they have three or four seasons to watch. They're all fans, it's just some are more aggressive.

Fan differentiation becomes extra relevant in the age of the mega-convention. Given that 130,000 people now attend San Diego Comic-Con and thousands are descending on smaller conventions like Gallifrey One (which just five years ago had half that number), Emily notes how big conventions will split into cliques: "When I go to Comic-Cons, it's almost a little more like high school lunch table clique to me. So you have the Homestucks, who all hang out together, they're all in those costumes. I see all the comic book characters, hanging out together—like Marvel Universe, DC Universe. The Whovians stay together, but they're always near the Supernatural and the Sherlockian." Valoise also talks about big conventions being dominated by old, white males: "You've got the guys, the crusty old coots who have been going since the 50s and they resent those crazy kids who won't get off their lawn!"

Finally, both Pat and Cinnamon noted intra-fandom dissonance related to their fannish objects (*Sherlock* and *Doctor Who*, respectively). Within *Doctor Who* fandom, there was much discussion of the newly female Master character (the Master, as a Time Lord, can regenerate and for the first time, the character became a woman). Cinnamon thinks that "online, people like to butcher each other whether there should be a female Master—people get so passionate about it." For Pat, a longtime Sherlockian, the problem with *Sherlock* fandom was the influx of new fans: "there's a little bit of tension from people who have been around before, we feel protective of the characters." She is referring her specifically to Sherlock and his portrayal by Cumberbatch, and the influx of fans "sometimes [think] their priority is him, as an actor and as a person, and not necessarily on the integrity on keeping the Holmesian universe."

Fan antagonism in the *SuperWhoLock* world is not unusual, but I should note it is also not egregious. Almost all the fans I spoke with equivocated at points in their discussion—"it's just what I've read," or "it's just a stereotype." By and large, most of the fans felt as Ben did:

> I think there's an underlying respect [between these fandoms]. … But you go to see some conventions and … the fans have this rivalry going on. And for me I've never really experienced that, in terms of *Sherlock* and *Doctor Who*. And that's the same over here and in the US, I've found. … It's a nice fandom to be involved with.

Perhaps *SuperWhoLock* is a natural consequence of the presence and popularity of these three fandoms on Tumblr combined with the conversational nature of the fan interaction. With direct reference to one, eventually the conversation turns to the other three; a reference to one becomes imbued with the significance of all. Perhaps *SuperWhoLock* is not just about the fans of these three shows, but about the way fandom itself molds and changes to fit the environment, and the way fans move between texts, communities, and media with determination and intent. *SuperWhoLock* is certainly not going to last forever, but as a symbol of what it means to be a fan, it will help define a generation.

Conclusion

In Fig. 5.2, the *SuperWhoLock* fan artist has created—as we have seen illustrated time and again—a link between *Doctor Who* (upper left), *Supernatural* (upper right), and *Sherlock* (bottom right). To this connection, she has also added *Harry Potter* (bottom left), creating a sort of *SuperWhoPotterLock* connection between these texts. The link here is obvious: each show is connected via the phrase "everything is going to be ok," the underlying message this fan has taken from the four texts and applied to each one. Supporting her points (citationally), she applies a quotation from each of the four texts that demonstrate the "everything will be OK" argument. The *SuperWhoPotterLock* connection is held together by the theme of redemption and reassurance, a theme repeated throughout each of these texts multiple times. The Doctor, Sherlock, Harry Potter, and the Winchester brothers are redeemed more times than can be numbered;

Fig. 5.2 Everything Is Going to Be OK, by romangodfrey (http://romangodfrey.tumblr.com/post/44150676692/when-people-turn-to-fictional-characters-its)

they use their powers of reassurance just as often to convince their friends and followers of their worth and value. Her post was enormously popular with over 555,500 notes/shares/reblogs from other fans.

It is significant that these themes find their way into fandom, as fans often rely on their show for solace, comfort, and reassurance. While Zubernis and Larsen illustrate persuasively that fandom itself is a community that "builds confidence and self-esteem, offers a support system, and creates a space where people can explore and grow more comfortable with their identity," so too can the television texts themselves offer comfort and companionship to some who may be outside traditional community.[35] Fans can turn to their favorite texts to evoke certain emotions: I know what episode of *Doctor Who* I might put on if I am in a celebratory mood, a depressed mood, or an angry mood. Fandom may be a *community*, but it is also a profound *personal* connection to the text.

Importantly, this is reflected in the fan artists' depiction: instead of comforting their partner/companion/friend in these images, the protagonist is comforting *the same image* of a woman, composed in monochrome and drawn with far less detail than the main figures. The image was originally one GIF where the image of the woman remained static while the different protagonists flickered in and out of the frame. The sketched outline of the woman in the image becomes symbolic of fans themselves. Each fan is positioned in the images as the object of the media texts' reassurance: the Doctor implores, Harry holds, Sherlock comforts, Dean kisses. At the end of the day, this image seems to imply, when everything seems bleak and the world dark, dreary, and empty, there will still be things to look forward to; there will still be adventure, and family, and intelligence, and honor—and love.

This is *SuperWhoLock* fandom. Despite the antagonism, despite the rivalry, the underlying passion that fans feel for these three shows carries through in all the fiction, all the art, all the GIFs, and all the discussion. At the end of the day, fans have created with *SuperWhoLock* a unique fan-brand that integrates not only the three texts at the center, but also the fandoms themselves. Each *SuperWhoLock* is a unique reading of the combination of the three texts and these three fandoms. As I have described in this book, *SuperWhoLock* is held together by a sort of intra-transmediation, a bonding of internal characteristics that coheres the disparate texts within one corpus. But of course the sum of the parts is not the whole, nor is it cohesive. Each *SuperWhoLock* is different and utilizes a different reading of the source material.

Fandom in the twenty-first century is the same: every fan experiences and communicates their fandom in a unique way. That the media industries are commodifying fan activities and communities into particular ways and strategies of being may create the appearance of an homogenous and mainstream fandom.[36] Indeed, for fandom to become mainstream, it must appear as through it is funneled into a particular identity. Yet, the existence of *SuperWhoLock* and other fan-created texts (*Inspector Spacetime*, Questarians, et al.) demonstrates that fans are still working outside the industry. Were *SuperWhoLock* to become "canon" in any of the three shows (or, more accurately, in all of the three shows), I suspect its draw would significantly lessen.

In other words, the appeal of *SuperWhoLock* may certainly include the attractiveness of the male leads, the similarities between the shows, the comfort provided to the fans, the engaging writing, the intelligence, the adventure, the humor—but more than anything I think the appeal lies in its very alienness. It fits…but also kind of does not fit at all. It is not like a crossover between two or three *CSI* or *Law and Order* series, which all take place in a supposed "real world" and all feature mundane plots. *SuperWhoLock* works precisely because it does not, and that possibility within the impossibility resonates within *Supernatural*, *Doctor Who*, and *Sherlock*. As a fan-created text, as a crossover universe that can never be, *SuperWhoLock* exists at the periphery of imagination, and at the center of fandom.

Notes

1. Jenkins, *Textual Poachers*, 170–1.
2. Johnson, "Fan-tagonism"; Hills, "'Twilight' Fans"; Busse, "Geek Hierarchies"; Stanfill, "Intra-Fandom Stereotyping"; Williams, 'Muse'; Dare-Edwards, "Fangirl Identity."
3. Stanfill, "Intra-Fandom Stereotyping," 124.
4. Dare-Edwards, "Fangirl Identity."
5. Booth, *Playing Fans*, 26–7.
6. Polasek, "Winning," 46.
7. Karkanias, "The Intra- and Inter-Sub-Community Dynamics of Fandom," 1.
8. Hills, "'Twilight' Fans."
9. Stanfill, "Intra-Fandom Stereotyping," 120.
10. Busse, "Geek Hierarchies," 78.
11. Stanfill, "Intra-Fandom Stereotyping," 129.
12. Hills, "'Twilight' Fans," 123.
13. Hills, "'Twilight' Fans," 114, 125–6.
14. Dare-Edwards, "Fangirl Identity," citing Busse, "Geek Hierarchies"; Hills, "'Twilight' Fans"; Williams, "'Muse."
15. Gray, "Antifandom," 841.
16. Williams, 'Muse'; Stanfill, "Intra-Fandom Stereotyping"; Hills, "'Twilight' Fans"; Karkanias, "The Intra- and Inter-Sub-Community Dynamics of Fandom."
17. Jones, "*My Little Pony*," 121.
18. Hills, "'Twilight' Fans," 114, 121–2.
19. Williams, 'Muse,' 335.

20. Karkanias, "The Intra- and Inter-Sub-Community Dynamics of Fandom," 13–14.
21. Zubernis and Larsen, *Fandom at the Crossroads*, 118.
22. Dare-Edwards, "Fangirl Identity."
23. Zubernis and Larsen, *Fandom at the Crossroads*, 119–20.
24. Karkanias, "The Intra- and Inter-Sub-Community Dynamics of Fandom," 14.
25. Hillman, Procyk, and Neustaedter, "'alksjdf;lksfd.'"
26. Stanfill, "Intra-Fandom Stereotyping," 124.
27. Hills, "'Twilight' Fans."
28. Williams, 'Muse,' 334.
29. Harman and Jones, "Fifty Shades of Ghey," 951–68.
30. Not her real name.
31. Stanfill, "Intra-Fandom Stereotyping," 118, 123, 125–7.
32. Booth, *Playing Fans.*
33. Not her real name.
34. Hills, "'Twilight' Fans," 123.
35. Zubernis and Larson, *Fandom at the Crossroads*, 87.
36. Booth, *Playing Fans*; Coppa, "Fuck Yeah."

Bibliography

Arvidsson, Adam. 2006. *Brands: Meaning and value in media culture*. London: Routledge.

Åström, Berit. 2010. 'Let's get those Winchesters pregnant': Male pregnancy in *Supernatural* fan fiction. *Transformative Works and Cultures* 4. http://dx.doi.org/10.3983/twc.2010.0135.

Bacon-Smith, Camile. 1992. *Enterprising women: Television fandom and the creation of popular myth*. Philadelphia: University of Pennsylvania Press.

Banash, David. 2013. Virtual life and the value of objects: Nostalgia, distinction and collecting in the twenty-first century. In *Contemporary collecting: Objects, practices, and the fate of things*, ed. Kevin M. Moist and David Banash, 55–66. Lanham: Scarecrow Press.

Basu, Balaka. 2012. *Sherlock* and the (Re)invention of modernity. In *Sherlock and transmedia fandom*, ed. Louisa Ellen Stein and Kristina Busse, 196–209. Jefferson: McFarland.

Beattie, Melissa. 2013. The 'Doctor Who Experience' (2012–) and the commodification of Cardiff Bay. In *New dimensions of Doctor Who*, ed. Matt Hills, 175–189. London: I.B. Tauris.

Bennett, Tony, and Janet Woollacott. 1984. *Bond and beyond: The political career of a popular hero*. London: Routledge.

Bochman, Svetlana. 2014. Sherlock Holmes, tech-geek: Uncovering new media's significance in "Sherlock", the BBC's modern adaptation of Conan Doyle's stories. *The Victorian* 2(1): 1–17.

Booth, Paul. 2008. Rereading fandom: MySpace character personas and narrative identification. *Critical Studies in Media Communication* 25(5): 514–536.

P. Booth, *Crossing Fandoms*, DOI 10.1057/978-1-137-57455-8

Booth, Paul. 2010. *Digital fandom: New media studies*. New York, NY: Peter Lang.

Booth, Paul. 2012. *Time on TV: Temporal displacement and mashup television*. New York, NY: Peter Lang.

Booth, Paul. 2013a. The first time. In *Fan phenomena: Doctor Who*, ed. Paul Booth, 72–82. Bristol: Intellect.

Booth, Paul. 2013b. Reifying the fan: Inspector Spacetime as fan practice. *Popular Communication* 11(2): 146–159.

Booth, Paul. 2013c. The cultural lives of *Doctor Who*: Celebrations, conferences, conventions. *Antenna*, 3 December 2013. http://blog.commarts.wisc.edu/2013/12/03/the-cultural-lives-of-doctor-who-celebrations-conferences-conventions/. Accessed 30 Sept 2015.

Booth, Paul, ed. 2013d. *Fan phenomena: Doctor Who*. Bristol, UK: Intellect.

Booth, Paul. 2014. Periodising *Doctor Who*. *Science Fiction Film and Television* 7(2): 195–215.

Booth, Paul. 2015a. *Playing fans: Negotiating fandom and media in the digital age*. Iowa City, IA: University of Iowa Press.

Booth, Paul. 2015b. *Game play: Paratextuality in contemporary board games*. New York, NY: Bloomsbury.

Booth, Paul. 2016. *BioShock*: Rapture through transmedia. In *The rise of transtexts: Challenges and opportunities*, ed. Benjamin W.L. Derhy and Mélanie Bourdaa. London: Routledge.

Booth, Katie, and Paul Booth. 2014. The discourse of authenticity in the *Doctor Who* fan Community. In *The language of Doctor Who*, ed. Jason Barr and Camille D.G. Mustachio, 259–273. Lanham: Roman and Littlefield.

Booth, Paul, and Jef Burnham. 2014. Who are we? Re-envisioning the doctor in the 21st century. In *Remake television: Reboot, re-use, recycle*, ed. Carlen Lavigne, 203–220. Lanham: Lexington Books.

Booth, Paul, and Peter Kelly. 2013. The changing faces of *Doctor Who* fandom: New fans, new technologies, old practices? *Participations* 10(1). http://www.participations.org/Volume%2010/Issue%201/5%20Booth%20&%20Kelly%2010.1.pdf.

Booy, Miles. 2012. *Love and monsters: The Doctor Who experience, 1979 to the present*. London: I.B. Tauris.

Börzsei, Linda. 2012. Just playing in the sandbox: Fan identities from a play perspective. Research Paper for Game Studies in the New Media and Digital Culture Programme, Utrecht University. http://www.academia.edu/7928842/Just_Playing_in_the_Sandbox_Fan_Identities_from_a_Play_Perspective.

Bourdieu, Pierre. 1984. *Distinction: A social critique of the judgment of taste*. Cambridge: Harvard University Press. Translated by Richard Nice.

Bourdieu, Pierre. 1990. *The logic of practice*. Redwood City: Stanford University Press.

Brennan, Joseph. 2014. 'Fandom is full of pearl clutching old ladies': Nonnies in the online slash closet. *International Journal of Cultural Studies* 17(4): 363–380.

Briggs, Nicholas. 2011. Commentary on *The final problem.* London: Big Finish Audio.

Britton, Piers. 2011. *TARDISBound: Navigating the universes of Doctor Who.* London: I.B. Tauris.

Busse, Kristina. 2013. Geek hierarchies, boundary policing, and the gendering of the good fan. *Participations* 10(1): 73–91.

Busse, Kristina, and Karen Hellekson. 2006. Introduction: Work in progress. In *Fan fiction and fan communities in the age of the Internet*, ed. Karen Hellekson and Kristina Busse, 5–32. Jefferson: McFarland.

Busse, Kristina, and Louisa Ellen Stein. 2012. Conclusion: Transmedia Sherlock and beyond. In *Sherlock and transmedia fandom*, ed. Louisa Ellen Stein and Kristina Busse, 224–231. Jefferson: McFarland.

Byrne-Cristiano, Laura. 2013. The BBC and CW announce joint 'SuperWhoLock' show coming this fall. *Hypable.* 1 April 2013. http://www.hypable.com/superwholock-announced/. Accessed 29 Sept 2015.

Chapman, James. 2000. *Licence to thrill: A cultural history of the James Bond films.* London: I.B. Tauris.

Chapman, James. 2013. *Inside the TARDIS: The worlds of Doctor Who: A cultural history*, 2nd ed. I.B. London: I.B. Tauris, UK.

Church, David. 2015. *Grindhouse nostalgia: Memory, home video and exploitation film fandom.* Edinburgh: Edinburgh University Press.

Coppa, Francesca. 2006. Brief history of media fandom. In *Fan fiction and fan communities in the age of the Internet*, ed. Karen Hellekson and Kristina Busse, 41–61. Jefferson: McFarland Press.

Coppa, Francesca. 2012. Sherlock as cyborg: Bridging mind and body. In *Sherlock and transmedia fandom*, ed. Louisa Ellen Stein and Kristina Busse, 210–223. Jefferson: McFarland.

Coppa, Francesca. 2014. Fuck yeah, fandom is beautiful. *Journal of Fandom Studies* 2(1): 73–82.

Dare-Edwards, Helena. 2015. Negotiating a fangirl identity. Paper presented at Fan Studies Network symposium, Norwich, UK, June 2015.

De Kosnik, Abigail. 2009. Should fan fiction be free? *Cinema Journal* 48(4): 118–124.

De Souza e Silva, Adriana, and Daniel M. Sutko. 2011. Placing location-aware media in a history of the virtual. In *The long history of new media*, ed. David W. Park, Nicholas W. Jankowski, and Steve Jones, 299–316. New York: Peter Lang.

Doran, Sarah. 2015. Christopher Eccleston: Why my Doctor had to be northern. *Radio Times,* 14 April 2015. http://www.radiotimes.com/news/2015-04-

14/christopher-eccleston-why-my-doctor-had-to-be-northern. Accessed 30 Sept 2015.

Evans, Elizabeth Jane. 2012. Shaping Sherlocks: Institutional practice and the adaptation of character. In *Sherlock and transmedia fandom*, ed. Louisa Ellen Stein and Kristina Busse, 102–117. Jefferson: McFarland.

Faye, Lindsay. 2012. Prologue: Why Sherlock? Narrative investment in the BBC series. In *Sherlock and transmedia fandom*, ed. Louisa Ellen Stein and Kristina Busse, 1–8. Jefferson: McFarland.

Felschow, Laura. 2010. 'Hey, check it out, there's actually fans': (Dis)empowerment and (Mis)representation of cult fandom in *Supernatural. Transformative Works and Cultures* 4. http://dx.doi.org/10.3983/twc.2010.0134.

Fine, Gary Alan, and Lisa-Jo Van den Scott. 2011. Wispy communities: Transient gatherings and imagined micro-communities. *American Behavioral Scientist* 55(10): 1319–1335.

Fiske, John. 1992. The cultural economy of fandom. In *The adoring audience: Fan culture and popular media*, ed. Lisa A. Lewis, 30–49. London: Routledge.

Geraghty, Lincoln. 2007. *Living with Star Trek: American culture and the Star Trek universe.* London: I.B. Tauris.

Geraghty, Lincoln. 2014. *Cult collectors: Nostalgia, fandom and collecting popular culture.* New York: Routledge.

Godwin, Victoria. 2015. G.I. Joe Vs. Barbie: Anti-fandom, fashion, dolls, and one-sixth scale action figures. *Journal of Fandom Studies* 3(2): 119–133.

Goldthorpe, John H., and David Lockwood. 1963. Affluence and the British class structure. *The Sociological Review* 11(2): 133–163.

Gray, Jonathan. 2005. Antifandom and the moral text: Television without pity and textual dislike. *The American Behavioral Scientist* 48(7): 840–858.

Gunkel, David. 2008. Rethinking the digital remix: Mash-ups and the metaphysics of sound recording. *Popular Music and Society* 31(4): 489–510.

Harman, Sarah, and Bethan Jones. 2013. Fifty shades of ghey: Snark fandom and the figure of the anti-fan. *Sexualities* 16(8): 951–968.

Harrigan, Pat, and Noah Wardrip-Fruin. 2009. Introduction. In *Third person: Authoring and exploring vast narratives*, ed. Pat Harrigan and Noah Wardrip-Fruin, 1–9. Cambridge: MIT Press.

Harvey, C.B. 2012. Sherlock's webs: What the detective remembered from the doctor about transmediality. In *Sherlock and transmedia fandom*, ed. Louisa Ellen Stein and Kristina Busse, 118–132. Jefferson: McFarland.

Hellekson, Karen. 2009. A fannish field of value: Online fan gift culture. *Cinema Journal* 48(4): 113–118.

Hellekson, Karen. 2013. 'Doctor Who unbound', the alternate history and the fannish text. In *Fan phenomena: Doctor Who*, ed. Paul Booth, 128–135. Bristol: Intellect.

Hewett, Richard. 2014. Who is Matt Smith? Performing the Doctor. In *Doctor Who: The eleventh hour*, ed. Andrew O'Day, 13–30. London: I.B. Tauris.

Hibbard, James. 2015. *Doctor Who* movie, *Sherlock* crossover not happening, Steven Moffat Says. *Entertainment Weekly*, 2 April 2015. http://www.ew.com/article/2015/04/02/doctor-who-movie. Accessed 30 Sept 2015.

Hillman, Serena, Jason Procyk, and Carman Neustaedter. 2014. 'alksjdf;lksfd': Tumblr and the fandom user experience. DIS'14, 21–25 June 2014, Vancouver, BC, Canada.

Hills, Matt. 2002. *Fan cultures.* London: Routledge.

Hills, Matt. 2003. Recognition in the eyes of the relevant beholder: Representing 'subcultural celebrity' and cult TV fan cultures. *Mediactive* 2(2): 59–73.

Hills, Matt. 2005a. Negative fan stereotypes ('Get a life!') and positive fan injunctions ('Everyone's got to be a fan of something!'): Returning to hegemony theory in fan studies. *Spectator* 25(1): 35–47.

Hills, Matt. 2005b. Patterns of surprise: The 'Aleatory object' in psychoanalytic ethnography and cyclical fandom. *American Behavioral Psychologist* 48(7): 801–821.

Hills, Matt. 2010. *Triumph of a time lord: Regenerating Doctor Who in the twenty-first century.* London, UK: I.B. Tauris.

Hills, Matt. 2012a. *Sherlock*'s epistemological economy and the value of 'fan' knowledge: How producer-fans play the (great) game of fandom. In *Sherlock and transmedia fandom*, ed. Louisa Ellen Stein and Kristina Busse, 27–40. Jefferson: McFarland.

Hills, Matt. 2012b. Torchwood's trans-transmedia: Media tie-ins and brand 'fanagement'. *Participations: The Journal of Audience and Reception Studies* 9(2): 409–428.

Hills, Matt. 2012c. 'Twilight' fans represented in commercial paratexts and inter-fandoms: Resisting and repurposing negative fan stereotypes. In *Genre, reception, and adaptation in the Twilight series*, ed. Anne More, 113–131. Farnham: Ashgate.

Hills, Matt. 2013. The cultural lives of Doctor Who: What's special about multiple multi-doctor specials? *Antenna*, 15 October 2013. http://blog.commarts.wisc.edu/2013/10/15/the-cultural-lives-of-doctor-who-whats-special-about-multiple-multi-doctor-specials/. Accessed 30 Sept 2015.

Hills, Matt. 2014. From Dalek half balls to Daft Punk helmets: Mimetic fandom and the crafting of replicas. *Transformative Works and Cultures* 16. http://dx.doi.org/10.3983/twc.2014.0531.

Hills, Matt. 2015a. *Doctor Who: The unfolding event: Marketing, merchandising and mediatizing a brand anniversary.* Houndmills: Palgrave.

Hills, Matt. 2015b. Fandom as an object and the objects of fandom, interview with Clarice Greco. *Matrize* 9(1): 147–163.

Hills, Matt. 2015c. Doctor Who's travels in space and time with BBC worldwide: Fantasizing/protecting a 'British' brand in the US? Presented at the Society for Cinema Studies conference, Montreal, CA, April 2015.

Jamison, Anne. 2013. *Fic: Why fanfiction is taking over the world*. Dallas: BenBella.

Jenkins, Henry. 1992. *Textual poachers: Television fans and participatory culture*. New York: Routledge.

Jenkins, Henry. 2006. *Convergence culture: Where old and new media collide*. New York: New York University Press.

Jenkins, Henry. 2007. Afterword: The future of fandom. In *Fandom: Identities and communities in a mediated world*, ed. Jonathan Gray, Cornel Sandvoss, and C. Lee Harrington, 357–364. New York: New York University Press.

Jenkins, Henry. 2011. Transmedia 202: Further reflections. *Confessions of an Aca-Fan,* 1 August 2011. http://henryjenkins.org/2011/08/defining_transmedia_further_re.html. Accessed 30 Sept 2015.

Jensen, Joli. 1992. Fandom as pathology: The consequences of characterization. In *The adoring audience*, ed. Lisa A. Lewis, 9–29. New York: Routledge.

Johnson, Derek. 2007. Fan-tagonism: Factions, institutions, and constitutive hegemonies of fandom. In *Fandom: Identities and communities in a mediated world*, ed. Jonathan Gray, Cornel Sandvoss, and C. Lee Harrington, 285–300. New York: New York University Press.

Jones, Bethan. 2015. *My Little Pony*, tolerance is magic: Gender policing and Brony anti-fandom. *Journal of Popular Television* 3(1): 119–125.

Karkanias, Alena. 2014. The intra- and inter-sub-community dynamics of fandom. Summer Research Paper 230. http://soundideas.pugetsound.edu/summer_research/230.

Kohnen, Melanie. 2015. 'The power of geek': Fandom as gendered commodity at comic-con. *Creative Industries Journal* 7(1): 75–78.

Kozinets, Robert V. 2014. Fan creep: Why brands suddenly need 'fans'. In *Wired TV: Laboring over an interactive future*, ed. Denise Mann, 161–175. New Brunswick: Rutgers.

Lamerichs, Nicolle. 2010. Stranger than fiction: Fan identity in cosplay. *Transformative Works and Cultures* 7. doi:10.3983/twc.2011.0246.

Lamerichs, Nicolle. 2012. Holmes abroad: Dutch fans interpret the famous detective. In *Sherlock and transmedia fandom*, ed. Louisa Ellen Stein and Kristina Busse, 179–195. Jefferson: McFarland.

Lamerichs, Nicolle. 2014. Embodied fantasy: The affective space of anime conventions. In *The Ashgate research companion to fan cultures*, ed. Linda Duits, Koos Zwaan, and Stijn Reijnders, 263–274. Farnham: Ashgate.

Larsen, Katherine, and Lynn Zubernis. 2013. *Fangasm: Supernatural fangirls*. Iowa City: University of Iowa Press.

Lausch, Kayti Adaire. 2013. The niche network: Gender, genre, and the CW brand. MA thesis, University of Texas-Austin. https://repositories.lib.utexas.

edu/bitstream/handle/2152/22453/LAUSCH-THESIS-2013.pdf?sequence=1.

Lavigne, Carlen. 2012. The Noble Bachelor and the Crooked Man. In *Sherlock Holmes for the 21st century: Essays on new adaptations*, ed. Lynnette Porter, 13–23. Jefferson: McFarland.

Lury, Celia. 2004. *Brands: The logos of the global economy*. London: Routledge.

Marshall, Kelli. 2011. Animated GIFs, cinemagraphs, and our return to early cinema. *Kelli Marshall*, 8 June 2011. http://kellimarshall.net/my-blog/best-of/animated-gifs/. Accessed 28 Aug 2013.

McClellan, Ann. 2014. Redefining genderswap fan fiction: A *Sherlock* case study. *Transformative Works and Cultures* 17. http://dx.doi.org/10.3983/twc.2014.0553.

MikeDimayua. SuperWhoLock, 2013. http://mikedimayuga.deviantart.com/art/Superwholock-374767844. Accessed 4 Jan 2016.

Moor, Liz. 2007. *The rise of brands*. Oxford: Berg.

Morris, Dylan. 2013. Britain as fantasy: New series *Doctor Who* in young American nerd culture. In *Fan phenomena: Doctor Who*, ed. Paul Booth, 50–61. Bristol: Intellect.

Navarro, Zander. 2006. In search of cultural interpretation of power: The contribution of Pierre Bourdieu. *IDS Bulletin* 37(6): 11–22.

Needless Procedures. 14 Jan 2012. http://hoursago.tumblr.com/post/15844762950/i-want-to-get-in-on-this-team-free-willteam. Accessed 4 Jan 2016.

Newman, Kim. 2008. *Doctor Who (BFI classics)*, 2nd ed. London: British Film Institute.

Noppe, Nele. 2011. Why we should talk about commodifying fan work. *Transformative Works and Cultures* 8. doi:10.3983/twc.2011.0369.

obsession_inc. 2009. Affirmational fandom vs. transformational fandom. 1 June 2009. http://obsession-inc.dreamwidth.org/82589.html. Accessed 21 Aug 2013.

Pearson, Roberta. 1997. 'It's always 1895': Sherlock Holmes in cyberspace. In *Trash aesthetics: Popular culture and its audience*, ed. Cartmell Deborah, I.Q. Hunter, Heidi Kaye, and Imelda Whelehan, 143–161. London: Pluto Press.

Pearson, Roberta. 2007. Bachies, Bardies, Trekkies, and Sherlockians. In *Fandom: Identities and communities in a mediated world*, ed. Jonathan Gray, Cornel Sandvoss, and C. Lee Harrington, 98–109. New York: New York University Press.

Pearson, Roberta. 2010. Fandom in the digital era. *Journal of Popular Communication* 8: 1–12.

Penley, Constance. 1992. Feminism, psychoanalysis, and the study of popular culture. In *Cultural studies*, ed. Lawrence Grossberg, Cary Nelson, and Paula A. Treichler, 479–500. New York: Routledge.

Perez, Nistasha. 2013. GIF fics and the rebloggable canon of *SuperWhoLock*. In *Fan phenomena: Doctor Who*, ed. Paul Booth, 148–157. Bristol: Intellect.

Perryman, Neil. 2008. *Doctor Who* and the convergence of media: A case study in transmedia storytelling. *Convergence: The International Journal of Research into New Media Technologies* 14(1): 21–39.

Polasek, Ashley D. 2012. Winning 'The grand game': *Sherlock* and the fragmentation of fan discourse. In *Sherlock and transmedia fandom*, ed. Louisa Ellen Stein and Kristina Busse, 41–55. Jefferson: McFarland.

Porter, Lynnette. 2012. *The Doctor Who franchise: American influence, fan culture and the spinoffs*. Jefferson: McFarland.

Porter, Lynnette. 2013. *Benedict Cumberbatch, in transition: An unauthorised performance biography*. London: MX Publishing.

Pullen, Kirsten. 2006. *The Lord of the Rings* online blockbuster fandom: Pleasure and commerce. In *The Lord of the Rings: Popular culture in global context*, ed. Ernest Mathijs, 172–188. London: Wallflower Press.

Romano, Aja. 2012. WTF is *SuperWhoLock? Daily Dot*, 5 October 2012. http://www.dailydot.com/entertainment/superwholock-fandom-supernatural-sherlock/. Accessed 30 Sept 2015.

Romano, Aja. 2014a. Chinese authorities are arresting writers of slash fanfiction. *Daily Dot*, 18 April 2014. http://www.dailydot.com/geek/in-china-20-people-women-arrested-for-writing-slash/. Accessed 30 Sept 2015.

Romano, Aja. 2014b. Why does the man behind 'Doctor Who' and 'Sherlock' still have a job? *Daily Dot*, 13 January 2014. http://www.dailydot.com/opinion/steven-moffat-sexism-sherlock-doctor-who/. Accessed 28 Dec 2015.

Sandifer, Phil. 2012. You were expecting someone else 9 (Longleat, Doctor Who monthly, the Peter Davison comics). *Tardis Eruditorum*, 2 April 2012. http://www.philipsandifer.com/blog/you-were-expecting-someone-else-9-longleat-doctor-who-monthly-the-peter-davison-comics/. Accessed 30 Sept 2015.

Sandvoss, Cornel. 2005. *Fans: The mirror of consumption*. Malden: Polity Press.

Sandvoss, Cornel. 2007. The death of the reader? Literary theory and the study of texts in popular culture. In *Fandom: Identities and communities in a mediated world*, ed. Jonathan Gray, Cornel Sandvoss, and C. Lee Harrington, 19–32. New York: New York University Press.

Schmidt, Lisa. 2010. Monstrous melodrama: Expanding the scope of melodramatic identification to interpret negative fan responses to *Supernatural*. *Transformative Works and Cultures* 4 . http://dx.doi.org/10.3983/twc.2010.0152.

Scott, A.O. 2015. At comic-con, bring out your fantasy and fuel the culture. *New York Times*, 15 July 2015. http://www.nytimes.com/2015/07/19/movies/at-comic-con-bring-out-your-fantasy-and-fuel-the-culture.html. Accessed 19 July 2015.

Scott, Suzanne. 2009. Repackaging fan culture: The regifting economy of ancillary content models. *Transformative Works and Cultures* 3. http://dx.doi.org/10.3983/twc.2009.0150.

Scott, Suzanne. 2013. Who's steering the mothership? Fanboy auteur in transmedia storytelling. In *The participatory culture handbook*, ed. Aaron Delwiche and Jennifer Henderson, 43–51. New York: Routledge.

Sheehan, Cassidy. 2015. Queer-baiting on the BBC's *Sherlock*: Addressing the invalidation of queer experience through online fan fiction communities. *Undergraduate Research Posters,* Poster 122. http://scholarscompass.vcu.edu/uresposters/122.

Smith, John. 2013. WHOLOCK- Sherlock meets the doctor! 11 December 2013. https://www.youtube.com/watch?v=q3bGYljQ5Uw. Accessed 4 Jan 2016.

Stanfill, Mel. 2013. 'They're losers, but I know better': Intra-fandom stereotyping and the normalization of the fan subject. *Critical Studies in Media Communication* 30(2): 117–134.

Stein, Louisa. 2015. *Millennial fandom: Television audiences in the transmedia age.* Iowa City: University of Iowa Press.

Stein, Louisa, and Kristina Busse. 2012. Introduction: The literary, televisual and digital adventures of the beloved detective. In *Sherlock and transmedia fandom*, ed. Louisa Ellen Stein and Kristina Busse, 9–24. Jefferson: McFarland Publishers.

Steward, Tom. 2012. Homes in the small screen: The television contexts of Sherlock. In *Sherlock and transmedia fandom*, ed. Louisa Ellen Stein and Kristina Busse, 133–149. Jefferson: McFarland.

Taylor, Rhonda Harris. 2012. A singular case of identity: Holmesian shapeshifting. In *Sherlock Holmes for the 21st century: Essays on new adaptations*, ed. Lynnette Porter, 93–113. Jefferson: McFarland.

Thomas, Angela. 2006. Fan fiction online. *Australian Journal of Language and Literacy* 29(3): 226–239.

Thomas, Lynne M. 2010. Marrying into the TARDIS tribe. In *Chicks dig Time Lords*, ed. Lynne M. Thomas and Tara O'Shea, 81–86. Des Moines: Mad Norwegian Press.

Tosenberger, Catherine. 2008. 'The epic love story of Sam and Dean': *Supernatural*, queer readings, and the romance of incestuous fan fiction. *Transformative Works and Cultures* 1. http://journal.transformativeworks.org/index.php/twc/article/view/30.

Tosenberger, Catherine. 2010. Love! Valor! Supernatural! [editorial]. *Transformative Works and Cultures* 4. http://dx.doi.org/10.3983/twc.2010.0212.

Tulloch, John, and Henry Jenkins. 1995. *Science fiction audiences: Watching Star Trek and Doctor Who.* New York: Routledge.

Tulloch, John, and Manuel Alvarado. 1984. *Doctor Who: The unfolding text*. New York: St. Martin's Press.

TWC Editor. 2010. Interview with Wincon organizer Ethrosdemon. *Transformative Works and Cultures* 4. http://dx.doi.org/10.3983/twc.2010.0208.

Uhlin, Graig. 2014. Playing in the gif(t) economy. *Games and Culture* 9(6): 517–527.

Watley, Erin. 2016. Race, gender, and digital media: *The Mis-Adventures of Awkward Black Girl* and representations of black female identity. In *Controversies in media ethics*, ed. Amber Davisson and Paul Booth, 248–263. New York: Bloomsbury.

Wilkinson, Jules. 2010. A box of mirrors, a unicorn, and a pony. *Transformative Works and Cultures* 4. http://dx.doi.org/10.3983/twc.2010.0159.

Williams, Rebecca. 2013. 'Anyone who calls Muse a *Twilight* band will be shot on sight': Music, distinction, and the 'interloping fan' in the *Twilight* franchise. *Popular Music and Society* 36(3): 327–342.

Zubernis, Lynn, and Katherine Larsen. 2012. *Fandom at the crossroads: Celebration, shame and fan/producer relationships*. Newcastle: Cambridge Scholars Press.

Index

P. Booth, *Crossing Fandoms*, DOI 10.1057/978-1-137-57455-8

CPSIA information can be obtained
at www.ICGtesting.com
Printed in the USA
LVHW080532141222
735193LV00004B/214

9 781137 574541